EthicsCentre CA
Canadian Centre for Ethics & Corporate Policy

Ethics & Governance:
Developing & Maintaining An Ethical Corporate Culture

Third Edition

Leonard J. Brooks
Professor of Business Ethics & Accounting
Executive Director, The Clarkson Centre for Business Ethics & Board Effectiveness
Rotman School of Management, University of Toronto

David Selley
Public Accountant
Past Chair, Canadian Centre for Ethics & Corporate Policy

Copyright © 2008
Canadian Centre for Ethics & Corporate Policy
Toronto, Canada
ISBN 978-0-9809641-0-3

Ethics & Governance: Developing & Maintaining An Ethical Corporate Culture

Contents

B. Governance Framework Requirements 135

Readings

Companion Website at http://www.ethicscentre.ca

Preface

The EthicsCentre CA was incorporated as a not-for-profit organization in 1988 with the legal name The Canadian Centre for Ethics & Corporate Policy. It was founded to champion the application of ethical values in the decision-making process of business and other organizations. Governed by volunteers and supported by organizations and individuals who share a commitment to ethical values, the Centre is dedicated to the promotion of an ethical orientation and culture in Canadian organizations.

The Centre fulfills its mission through a variety of activities which involve awareness building, learning, networking and referrals, collaborative relationships and the sponsoring of projects.

The publication of *Ethics & Governance: Developing and Maintaining an Ethical Corporate Culture* represents the successful conclusion of one of the Centre's more ambitious projects. The book is the result of the collaborative effort of two of the Centre's co-founders, Professor Leonard J. Brooks and David Selley, FCA. Professor Brooks is a Professor of Business Ethics & Accounting and Executive Director of The Clarkson Centre for Business Ethics & Board Effectiveness at the Rotman School of Management, University of Toronto. He has had a long and distinguished career in the business ethics field and is a recipient of the Ethics in Action Award for Ongoing Social Responsibility. David Selley spent his career at Ernst & Young (and its predecessor Clarkson Gordon), Chartered Accountants, where he specialized in auditing standards and methodologies. Since retirement, he has participated in various auditing projects for the Canadian Institute of Chartered Accountants and other organizations. A Past Chair of the Centre, he has also served on the board of Transparency International Canada.

The book is intended to serve as a practical resource for business. Providing support for the premise that an ethical corporate culture is essential for the ongoing success of a corporation and its executives, the authors then proceed to provide guidance on how to develop and effectively maintain such a corporate culture. The book includes checklists, tables and other helpful documents. A companion website provides up-to-date hotlinks, websites and readings that become relevant, thus keeping the guidance offered in the book current.

By publishing this book, the Directors of the Centre seek to contribute to the continuing conversation about ethics and good corporate governance for the benefit of its members and the broader business community.

Information about EthicsCentre CA and membership can be obtained by accessing its web site at www.ethicscentre.ca or contacting the Centre at 416-368-7525.

Hélène Yaremko-Jarvis, B.C.L., LL.B.
Executive Director
EthicsCentre CA

Understanding the Need for an Ethical Corporate Culture

Chapter 1
Introduction – Objectives, New Evidence, Overview

Recent corporate scandals have triggered a worldwide reform of corporate governance seeking to restore credibility to decision making, financial disclosure, and related financial markets. *Ethics & Governance: Developing & Maintaining an Ethical Corporate Culture* is dedicated to providing practical guidance to the core of governance reform – the development of a *culture of integrity*[1]. An accompanying website is provided by the Canadian Centre for Ethics & Corporate Policy at http://www.ethicscentre.ca for the posting of updates, news, and commentary on governance and ethics matters. Checklists, tables, and other helpful documents referenced in this book are available in downloadable format from the website.

The primary focus of this book is ethical conduct within companies,[2] particularly publicly traded corporations. Nevertheless, the material in this book is also relevant to any organization with even minimal public accountability, an array of stakeholders, or simply looking for ideas on how to instill ethics as part of the decision-making process. This material will also be useful, with very minor variations, to large public institutions such as hospitals, universities and other educational institutions, charitable organizations including NGOs, as well as private companies of all sizes, from large wholly-owned subsidiaries of major corporations to small owner-managed businesses. In particular, boards of directors of charitable organizations have strict fiduciary responsibilities, and history tells us that

---

1. See, for example, Jim Goodfellow and Allan Willis, "CEO Challenge," *CAmagazine* 40:1 (2007): 35–42.
2. Use of the term "company(ies)" or "organization(s)" throughout this book encompasses all forms of organization including for-profit and not-for-profit corporations, partnerships, and co-operatives. More specific terms are used when the context requires it.

such organizations are by no means immune from ethical problems, including employee fraud.

It is vital to note that many successful corporations have benefited from instilling *a culture of integrity* long before the Enron, Arthur Andersen, and WorldCom scandals triggered the *Sarbanes-Oxley Act of 2002* (SOX) and similar legislation and guidelines in Canada and other jurisdictions. They had been motivated to take a leading edge position on integrity or ethics by one or more of the following reasons:

- Good ethics are good business.
- Good ethics can support a competitive advantage.
- The enthusiastic support of some employees, customers, and other stakeholders depends on a culture of integrity.
- Employees at all levels, and company agents, need guidance about values or integrity expectations to make decisions that protect and further the company's strategic objectives.
- Company reputation and future profits depend significantly on demonstrating good corporate values.
- Sound risk management is based on ethical principles.

Governance reform has introduced the need for compliance with legislation such as SOX, and has forced CEOs and CFOs, as well as directors to make sure that their company's internal controls are adequate to protect the company and ensure that financial reports are accurate. Consequently, good governance requirements and expectations now require an assessment of a company's culture of integrity to be part of the risk management and internal control review processes. Moreover, many Canadian companies, and their auditors, are subject to SOX and SEC regulations, and Canadian securities regulators have formulated regulations that adopt certain, but not all, elements of this U.S. regulatory environment.

New Evidence

Recently published studies have underscored how important an ethics program leading to the development and maintenance of an ethical corporate culture is to the ongoing success of a corporation and its executives. For example, *KPMG's Ethics Survey, 2005–2006*[3] compares corporations

---

3. KPMG Forensic, *Integrity Survey 2005–2006* (KPMG LLP, 2005), downloadable from http://www.us.kpmg.com/services/content.asp?11id=10&12id=30&cid=1972 or http://www.us.kpmg.com/news/index.asp?cid=2051.

with and without an ethics program and finds that *an ethics program improves perceptions or behaviour* as follows:

- 6–12% reduction in observed misconduct or violation of values and principles in the prior 12 months
- 9–16% improvement in prevention of misconduct
- 39–48% improvement in comfort in reporting misconduct to a supervisor
- 27–46% improvement in belief that appropriate action will follow reporting of misconduct
- 43–54% improvement in perception that CEO and other top executives set the right "tone at the top"
- 37–49% improvement in motivation to "do the right thing"

Another example that focuses on the leadership role of the CEO, executives, and managers is research[4] that finds that to be perceived to be an ethical leader an individual must speak out about and demonstrate the ethical values the corporation or organization expects. If this is not done, employees will take the view that the only value that matters is making a profit. If the executives or leaders are silent on ethical matters, even if they are personally ethical, their reputation will be at considerable risk, as will be the corporation's.

There are still some executives and directors, as well as shareholders, who prefer to focus on making profits without making efforts to determine whether they are made ethically, or even legally. Such decision makers do not appreciate the potential damage that may be caused in the long run by failing to consider the strategic significance of consistently making ethical decisions. With the increasing complexity and rising pace of operations in business, even greater reliance will be placed on building relationships and managing risks ethically; which will require increasing attention on developing an additional point of reference for decision making – an ethical corporate culture to guide employees to behave ethically.

Overview of the Book

Chapter 2 provides insights into what constitutes an ethical culture, and

---

4. Linda Klebe Treviño, Laura Pincus Hartman, Michael Brown, "Moral Person and Moral Manager: How Executives Develop A Reputation for Ethical Leadership," *California Management Review* 42 (2000): 128–142.

expands on why a culture of integrity is desirable. The following questions are specifically discussed:

- What constitutes an ethical culture, and how does it work?
- What considerations or values define an ethical culture?
- Why is a culture of integrity needed?

The chapter refers to Appendix B which outlines the impact of regulation, notably SOX, SEC, Canadian, and stock exchange guidance, on corporate governance and ethical requirements.

Chapter 3 follows with practical insights into how to establish an effective ethical culture. Specific segments will cover:

- Creating a governance and leadership framework
- Motivating leaders
- Developing the core values and issues foundation

Chapter 4 offers insights for creating the guidance communications and framework including the mission statement, code of conduct, and other decision aids; and for developing commitment to, and understanding of, the organization's ethical objectives by:

- Integration of core values into strategic objectives and operational goals
- Effective communication of values
- Building on input from all levels

Chapter 5 reviews how to launch a new ethical corporate culture successfully in order to develop understanding and commitment to its principles.

Chapter 6 is focussed on how organizations can work towards ongoing reinforcement of the organization's values and preferred practices, and on encouraging compliance with its policies. Techniques discussed include:

- Reinforcement of values
- Communication and feedback mechanisms
- Ombudsmen, hotlines, whistle-blower programs, and inquiry services

Chapter 7 provides options for monitoring and reporting ethical performance, as well as Corporate Social Responsibility (CSR), which is a subject of growing interest for many organizations under pressure for transparency from external stakeholders Issues examined include:

- What does CSR mean, and how does it relate to ethical performance
- What frameworks for CSR measurement are being developed
- Where to look for comparators
- The audit of CSR reports

Chapter 8 presents several approaches to ethical decision making, which is a vital part of an ethical corporate culture since it protects the organization's values and reputation, and if proper techniques are applied correctly, leaves the executives and employees in a defensible position.

Chapters 9 and 10 deal with the important problems posed by conflicts of interest and international operations. Both are challenging, and companies need to consider carefully how they will deal with the ethical risks inherent in each area.

Chapter 11 indicates how the issues discussed and suggestions made in this book can be applied to not-for-profit entities and small owner-managed enterprises. Not surprisingly, all that is covered should be understood by the leaders of these organizations, and most of the content of this book is equally applicable, or more so.

In addition to the commentary in each Chapter, very useful readings, and a series of case commentaries are offered to outline, clarify, and illuminate issues causing or involved in important ethical problems facing corporations.

Finally, an accompanying website is available at http://www.ethicscentre.ca, where postings will be made of updates, news, useful websites, and commentary on governance and ethics matters. Checklists and other helpful forms referenced in this book are available in downloadable form from the website.

The End of the Beginning

More executives and directors are beginning to understand that corporations are now accountable to shareholders *and other stakeholders*, and that leading companies have responded, thus shifting expectations for all corporations. Governance reform, triggered by scandals and introduced to restore corporate credibility and public confidence in capital markets, is now seen to depend on an ethical corporate culture that provides appropriate guidance for behaviour. Effective risk management, necessary to keep corporations on track, also depends upon an ethical corporate culture. Directors and senior executives must give adequate attention to the development and maintenance of an ethical corporate culture. Otherwise they must live with the personal vulnerability of inadequate due diligence, and/or failure to fully achieve strategic objectives.

Leonard J. Brooks
David Selley.

Understanding the Need for an Ethical Corporate Culture

Chapter 2
What is an ethical culture, and why have one?

Organizational Culture – Ethical Culture – Good Governance

The achievement of a corporation's strategic objectives cannot be left to chance. Directors are now expected to ensure that employees are given adequate guidance and encouragement so that they further the company's strategic performance while minimizing risk. Since the early 1990's, the realization has grown that the organization's culture is critical to the desired guidance and encouragement process. Without a supportive ethical culture[1] – a culture of integrity – even well-intentioned directors and executives cannot expect accurate financial reporting and ethical operations that will generate and maintain the support of key stakeholder groups. Without support from an *ethical corporate culture*, the achievement of strategic business objectives cannot be attained on a sustained basis.

An organization's culture is the set of beliefs, norms and practices that are shared by the organization's members[2]. Employee actions flow from beliefs and norms that are conditioned to a significant extent by those of the organization as defined in mission statements, codes, and other reinforcing communications, as well as those that are informally observed from existing practices. However, employee beliefs are also determined with reference to their personal values as well as those they believe are held by their managers, and motivated or rewarded by their company. This chain of influence is portrayed in Figure 2.1. Further details concerning how a cul-

---

1. Ethics have to do with deciding what is right and wrong, and an ethical corporate culture is one that encourages employees toward right rather than wrong behaviour.
2. Susan Key, "Organizational Ethical Culture: Real or Imagined?" *Journal of Business Ethics,* 20 (1999): 217–218.

Figure 2.1
Organizational Culture Influence Chain

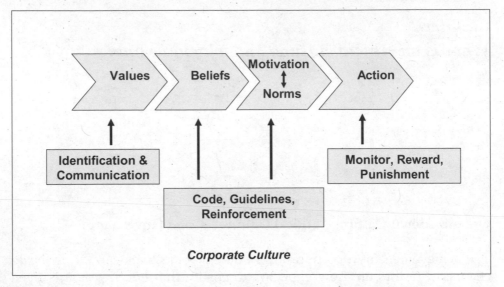

ture works are provided below, particularly in Part 2, "Establishing an Ethical Culture."

In 1982, in their classic book, *In Search of Excellence*, Peters and Waterman[3] identified how an organization's culture could contribute to success or failure by influencing the behaviour of the organization's members. Schein[4] followed in 1985 underscoring just how influential an organization's culture could be. Schein argued that culture is pervasive and consists of a set of shared values or assumptions that motivate behaviour, provide the key to understanding organizations, define leadership, and can be taught or modified by leaders who wish to create change. He goes on to explore the elements of culture and how the change process works. A very brief summary of his book is found at http://www.tnellen.com/ted/tc/schein.html.

Figure 2.2 illustrates key linkages of basic elements and reinforcers of an organizational culture, with the outcomes and impacts they can influence.

A properly thought out organizational culture provides a framework

3. Thomas J. Peters and Robert H. Waterman. *In Search of Excellence: Lessons from America's Best-Run Companies* (New York: Harper & Row, 1984, c1982).
4. Edgar H. Schein, *Organizational Culture and Leadership* (San Francisco: Jossey-Bass, 1985).

Figure 2.2
Organizational Culture, Individual/Team Outcomes, &
Organizational Effectiveness

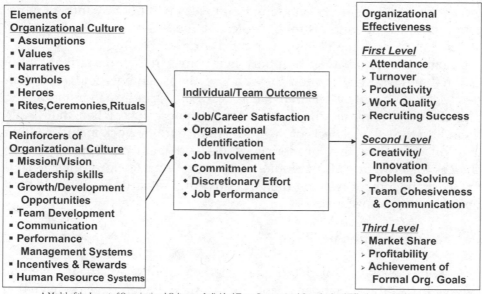

A Model of the Impact of Organizational Culture on Individual/Team Outcomes and Organizational Effectiveness, *The Business Case for Culture Change*. W. Reschke & R. Aldag, Center for Organizational Effectiveness, August 2000.

that motivates employee actions in accord with the organization's strategic goals. Values are a vital element of an organizational culture because they can define important behavioural principles, and therefore guide how employees will act with the organization's stakeholders. Given the potential gains and risks involved, it is surprising how few organizations have, until recently, given adequate attention to their culture and the choice of values that are most supportive of their strategic objectives.

However, while values are important core touchstones for the establishment of patterns of motivation, norms and behaviour, an effective ethical system of governance requires more than just signposts pointing in the right direction. Experience and recent research have found that just identifying and articulating a set of corporate values, even with rules for their implementation, do not guarantee their use. In fact, codes of conduct are often skeptically referred to as "ethical art" to emphasize their limited usefulness as wall decoration unless accompanied by other support and reinforcement mechanisms. In this respect, ethical values and rules are perhaps even harder than health and safety objectives to get employees to observe; primarily because the positive value of an *ethics program* is not as intuitively evident to employees. They may believe that non-ethical behaviour is in their self-interest and is profit maximizing for the corporation. To convince employees otherwise requires an all-out effort equivalent to that which would be mounted for a health and safety program or an environmental sensitivity program. Employees will not buy into an ethics program unless there is a strong, dedicated, well-resourced effort directed at developing and maintaining an ethical corporate culture.

Organizations embed and support their values in their narratives, publications, and speeches; when they choose their symbols and pick their heroes; and when they celebrate their successes. As indicated in Figure 2.2, organizations reinforce the importance of their values when they build them into the other aspects of their governance framework including their mission or vision, their leadership skills and team development, their choices for growth and development, their communications, their performance management systems, their incentive and reward systems, and their human resource systems.

Can an Organization be Ethical?

The values chosen will determine whether employees are directed to behave in an ethical manner or not. For example, if employees believe that profit is all-important and to be maximized at any cost, there is a significant probability that they will be led to step over the line and act unethically. This is because they will very likely offend one or more of the interests of the corporation's stakeholders during an unbalanced pursuit of the interests of shareholders. Current thinking is that *in order to attain its strategic objectives on a sustained basis, a corporation needs the support of at least its key stakeholder groups*, so taking account of stakeholder interests is very important. While it is not possible to please all of the stakeholders all of the time, it is short-sighted not to build a corporation's strategy and culture on a multiplicity of stakeholder interests. Moreover, *the degree to which a corporate culture is based on ethical principles that respect the rights of a multiplicity of stakeholders will determine its degree of ethicality*. A self-assessment score sheet to assess the degree to which stakeholder interests or rights are respected is available on the accompanying website at http://www.ethicscentre.ca.

An *ethical corporate culture* provides a common frame of reference that can influence the behaviour of a corporation's employees. It instills principles of management and control that lead to desirable ethical outcomes. It is based upon and defines the values or principles for which an organization stands and thus its identity. Essentially it involves (a) establishing a shared set of organizational values that support and encourage ethical

Figure 2.3
Key Stakeholder Support is Vital

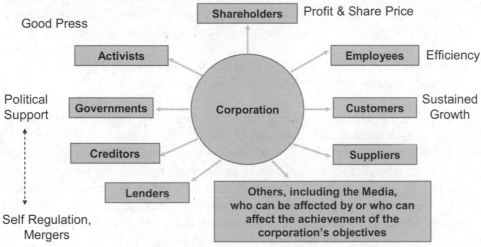

© 2007 L.J. Brooks.   Reproduced with permission from
Business & Professional Ethics for Directors, Executives & Accountants, Thomson South-Western

behaviour[5] and (b) integrating these values into the day-to-day activities of management and employees.

How to define and establish a corporation's values is covered in the next chapter, but many choose core values from such sources as:

- Reputation drivers[6] – trustworthiness, credibility, reliability, responsibility
- Hypernorms[7] – honesty, fairness, compassion, integrity, predictability, responsibility
- Ethical decision criteria[8] – net positive utility or consequences of an action; observance of duties, rights and/or fairness; and virtuosity expected

---

5. According to the *New Shorter Oxford Dictionary*, "ethics" refers to the moral principles by which any particular person is guided. "Ethical behaviour" is a term used herein to refer to activity or rules of conduct guided by moral conduct.

6. Charles J. Fombrun, *Reputation: Realizing Value from the Corporate Image* (Boston: Harvard Business School Press, 1996.

7. A hypernorm is a norm which is thought to be considered ethical in most cultures around the world. *See* T.L. Fort, "A Review of Donaldson and Dunfee's Ties That Bind: A Social Contracts Approach to Business Ethics," *Journal of Business Ethics* 28 (2000): 383–87.

8. These approaches to ethical decision making were outlined in the June 2004 Ethics Education Task Force Report of the Association to Advance Collegiate Schools of Business (AACSB), the world-wide accreditation body for business schools as recommendations for the education of business students, See http://www.aacsb.edu.

It is true that some would argue that a corporation cannot really be ethical and that it would be a waste of time to try to make it so. However, authors like Harvard's Lynn Sharp Paine, whose seminal article is summarized below and reproduced beginning on page xx, argue that corporations can be very successful in instilling an ethical corporate culture.

Summary: Lynn Sharp Paine, "Managing for Organizational Integrity," *Harvard Business Review* **(1994) March–April: 106–117.**

Paine set the stage in 1994 for current thinking on corporate ethics. Her article demolished the widely held idea at the time that ethics was a matter of personal scruples and that the company bore no responsibility for the actions of individuals working within it or, as she puts it, "Ethics, after all, has nothing to do with management. ... typically, unethical business practice involves tacit, if not explicit, co-operation of others and reflects the values, attitudes, beliefs, language, and behavioural patterns that define an organization's operating culture. Ethics is as much an organizational as a personal issue."

She also devastatingly dismissed a solely compliance-based approach as adequate to allow an organization to qualify as ethical. Legal compliance is not enough, she argues. "The law does not generally seek to inspire human excellence or distinction. It is no guide for exemplary behaviour – or even good practice."

She goes on to describe an ethical organization in more depth and provides examples from the public arena of ethical and unethical decisions by major corporations.

If there is one piece of reading that an aspiring ethics officer, or indeed any person with significant managerial responsibility should read, the Paine article is it.

Even those who argue that a corporation cannot really be ethical must recognize that the devotion to maximizing profit alone is focussed on a measure that is imperfect. Profit does not take into account many aspects of a corporation's impact. Externalities, for example, represent important dimensions of corporate activity that are often not properly or quickly reflected in normal, historical, financial reports. Pollution created by a corporation is not reflected as a cost in its reports unless they clean it up or recompense an injured party. On the other hand, scholarships paid to employees' children are reflected as a cost in the corporation's accounts, but the benefits are not. In recognition of this lack of reflection in traditional reports, corporations are creating other forms of reporting to capture their impact, such as environmental impact reports or corporate social responsibility statements – and they are taking externalities into their strategic planning processes. The claim that all a company has to do is concentrate solely on its bottom line is both strategically short-sighted and misguided.

Why is a corporate culture of integrity needed?

It's Good Business: Corporations, as noted above, have entered an era in which stakeholders expect that their interests will be taken into account in return for their support. Unless a corporation enjoys the fully-committed support of its employees, costs will be higher than needed or opportunities will be lost through low effort. Unless a corporation enjoys the support of its customers, it will lose sales or margin, and in extreme cases may face consumer boycotts. This recent recognition of the impact of stakeholder expectations, and the related awakening of stakeholders' recognition of their power to influence corporate behaviour, have changed the regime faced by corporations from accountability to shareholders alone to accountability to stakeholders, which includes shareholders. Given this change, *it is just good business to be ethical and to take a multiplicity of stakeholder interests into account when determining strategy and implementing corporate goals and a supportive culture.* For an example, refer to the following case of the Holland America Line, which emphasizes the advantages that can accrue from good employee relations.

Illustrative Case: Positive Effects of an Ethical Culture

Holland America Line operates a fleet of cruise ships with worldwide itineraries. It has a first class reputation and its crews are admired by all it's passengers.

Most of the crew, except for the senior officers, are from Indonesia or the Philippines. Crew members that come into contact with passengers are trained at a Holland America training facility in Indonesia (S/S Nieuw Jakarta). They learn the skills needed for their role, including the use of English. They do a tour of duty of up to one year and then get as much time off as they want with their family before applying to sign back on for another stint. During the tour of duty they work long hours for modest pay, but more than they would earn at home, and they are learning skills that stand them in good stead for their entire working lives. They get to see the world and some establish permanent friendships with passengers.

Travellers on Holland America ships constantly praise the skill, friendliness, and cheerfulness of the crews and Holland America thereby greatly benefits from repeat business.

Surely, Holland America's primary objective is not to be a beneficiary to Indonesians and Filipinos. Yet they obviously recognize that treating their crews fairly is good for business. Of course, there are complaints and injustices here and there. The food provided to the crew looks pretty good when described by the Executive Chef, although one wonders why so many hustle off to McDonald's whenever they have the opportunity in port. However, the purpose of this case is not to illustrate perfection, but simply to show that concern for, and fair treatment of, employees, especially in a service industry, can be a major factor in business success.

Enhancing Trust and Reputation: An ethical corporate culture does not just provide strictures for employees to stay within; it can improve the level of trust in an organization. This is vital to the smooth functioning of employee groups, to the sharing of ideas, and to the willingness and pace of employee adaptation to change. Outsiders are also able and willing to rely more heavily on organizations engendering a high level of trust – a circumstance that works in favour of companies, particularly when they need tolerance in time of crisis.

A 1999 *KPMG Business Ethics Survey* of senior executives in the public and private sectors concludes that chief executives see, "public demand for assurance of ethical practice in both the private and public sector as strong and increasing." In addition, respondents to the survey indicated that, "the most influential reason to invest resources in ethics initiatives was 'protection or enhancement of reputation.'"[9] As a result, corporations are increasingly recognizing that they need to understand stakeholder expectations and that their actions and communications to stakeholders must demonstrate that they have this understanding. More and more large international corporations are devoting considerable resources to considering ethical issues and to disclosing how they are addressing these issues.

New Benchmarks for Profitable Behaviour: Fortunately this attention to stakeholder interests does not need to undermine long-term corporate profits. Many examples exist where ethical behaviour has led to competitive advantage and success, for example:

- In retailing – Nike, Nestlé, Loblaw's green products
- In autos – Toyota's hybrid green cars
- In community support – payment to Cornwall for moving an operation.

---

9. Executive Briefing, *1999 KPMG Business Ethics Survey: Managing for Ethical Practice,* March 1999. See summary at http://www.bentley.edu/cbe/research/surveys/17.cfm

Corporate Citizenship and Corporate Social Responsibility: For many companies, the linkage between an ethical corporate culture and their *corporate citizenship* is well worth exploring. The view of both insider and outsider stakeholders is conditioned by the way the company's culture influences employees to deal with *corporate social responsibility (CSR)* issues and therefore influences *corporate social performance.* Directors, executives and managers should be aware that there are consulting services[10] in Canada, the United States of America, and the United Kingdom that measure and track such performance for investors and other activist stakeholders.

Awards are also given to companies with outstanding performance records[11]. Many companies are publishing their social goals and programs, environmental, community, health and safety, and related performance on their websites and in special purpose reports. Corporations such as Shell, BP, and Nike provide ready examples. Significant worldwide efforts are also being made to develop and beta test broad-disclosure frameworks[12] that go well beyond traditional financial reports to include environmental, social performance, and other disclosures of interest to stakeholders. The bottom line is that stakeholders who have a concern about an entity's business practices now, more than ever before, have the means to significantly impact a company's reputation and market share.

Evidence of the pervasiveness of stakeholder interest in an organization's practices is shown in "Appendix A: CSR and Sustainability Reports, Indexes, and Rankings" located at the end of the book and on the website http://www.ethicscentre.ca, which includes:

- 25 companies with recent CSR reports per the Global Reporting Initiative (GRI) website
- 10 companies included in the Jantzi Social Index of October 2007
- 100 companies included in The 2007 AccountAbility Ranking
- 30 companies with CSR reports and related website addresses
- Over 300 companies included in the Dow Jones Sustainability World Index October 2007

Stakeholder Expectations and Power Growth: Evidence of corporate social

---

10. For example: Kinder, Lydenberg & Domini & Co, Inc. in Boston, EthicScan Canada Limited and Jantzi Research in Toronto, and Ethical Investment Research Services (EIRIS) in London.
11. Awards are given from such organizations as: PRNews/GeorgeTown University at http://www.prnewsonline.com/awards/csr/, CICA at http://www.cica.ca, and the Global Responsibility Initiaitve at http://www.globalreporting.org
12. See for example: Triple Bottom Line Reporting by AccountAbility at http://www.accountability21.net/ and the Global Reporting Initiative (GRI) http://www.globalreporting.org/Home

responsibility has further reinforced the desire of stakeholders to exert their power over corporations to make a difference. These influence attempts are sometimes direct, sometimes through the media, and sometimes through ethical investment funds. Managers of these funds screen corporate activities before investments are placed, and press for changes during the period of investment. The rate of return of these ethical funds can be in the top quartile of mutual funds on a continuing basis, so making such choices does not result in diminished returns. A review of socially responsible investing and investments is available at http://www.sio.com.

Speed and Depth of News Reporting – No Secrets: Not only have the expectations of stakeholders and their ability to exert their influence increased, but the speed of reporting unethical acts has increased dramatically. With satellite communication of news, actions on the other side of the world are known worldwide virtually instantly. Moreover, there is an extremely high likelihood that information on acts hoped to be kept secret will leak out or be reported for revenge, or the satisfaction of ethical principles, either internally within a corporation or through an act of whistle-blowing in public. Whistle-blower protection laws that are becoming more common have reduced the whistle-blower's risks for such reporting, and have even added some inducement for coming forward.

Scandals Trigger Governance Reform: At the same time shareholders and other stakeholders, including directors, have witnessed corporate scandals of a size and impact never imagined; and the credibility of corporate governance and reporting and of the capital markets they draw on have been thrown into crisis. The recovery of credibility lost due to the Enron, WorldCom, and Arthur Andersen scandals required the enactment of the governance reforming Sarbanes-Oxley Act of 2002 (SOX) followed by regulations from the Canadian Securities Administrators. SOX and the U.S. Securities and Exchange Commission (SEC) regulations it spawned have been applied to all corporations wishing to solicit funds from the U.S. public and their subsidiaries, and has been emulated to varying degrees in other countries.

Personal and Corporate Liability Soar: In the post-Enron environment, personal and corporate legal liability for misdeeds has soared, and the preventative nature of a good governance system has been recognized by directors and shareholders. Leaving aside the good business aspect of a governance system that embodies an ethical corporate culture, the post-SOX governance framework laid out in SEC regulations, and extended in New York Stock Exchange guidelines, or Canadian Securities Administrators' Regulations and Toronto Stock Exchange (TSE/now TSX) guidelines, requires corporate directors more than ever to develop and monitor a sound governance structure that is based upon an ethical culture. The development of expectations for directors wishing to show due diligence in their oversight of corporate governance has been furthered by pronouncements on appropriate internal controls necessary to assure accurate accounting records and reports from the Canadian Institute of Chartered Accountants (CICA), the American Institute of Certified Public Accountants (AICPA), and the Public Company Accounting Oversight Board (PCAOB) which now sets auditing standards for SEC registrants. This governance and internal control framework is outlined in the "Appendix B: Governance Framework Requirements" located at the end of the book. The impact of these laws, regulations, and pronouncements is such that while some may consider the resulting new governance framework to be too far-reaching, costly, and perhaps futile, legally it must nevertheless be implemented.

Prevention Requires Diligent Risk Management: Proper risk management provides one of the most important reasons for introducing an effective governance system based on an ethical corporate culture. Even though some argue the attempt to eliminate 100 percent of unethical acts is not possible, the majority of employees can be induced to behave ethically, and it is good risk management practice to encourage them to do so. Forensic specialists have understood for many years that although 10–20 percent of employees will never bend the rules, steal, or commit a fraud, 10–20 percent will do so regardless of what is put in place to stop them. The remaining majority of employees (80–60 percent) will bend the rules, steal, or commit a fraud if they think they can get away with it. This suggests that the directors of a corporation who do not try to provide sound ethical guidance and related internal controls could be vulnerable to illicit acts from 80–90 percent of their employees. On the other hand, directors who ensure the soundness of ethical guidance and related internal controls can take comfort that they have done everything reasonably possible to reduce vulnerability to illicit acts by all but a determined 10–20 percent of their employees.

Altruism: Finally, there are executives and employees who believe in, or are more comfortable when "doing the right thing" or are proud to be associated with a corporation that demonstrates ethical values. Studies[13] have shown that MBAs from leading North American and European schools are reluctant to take interviews with corporations with questionable reputations or culture because these may cause them future embarrassment.

---

13. See for example, David B. Montgomery and Catherine A. Ramus, "Corporate Social Responsibility Reputation Effects on MBA Job Choice," GSB Research Paper # 1805, May 2003.

Employees have been known to leave employers that suffer loss of ethical reputation. Recruiting and retaining the best and the brightest employees is increasingly difficult unless sufficient care is given to the development and maintenance of ethical reputation through the safeguards afforded by an ethical corporate culture.

Conclusions

Developing an ethical corporate culture involves going beyond an approach to ethics that focuses merely on concern for compliance with the law – the level usually regarded as the minimum for ethical performance. It means, as stated by Lynn Sharp Paine in, "Managing for Organizational Integrity," holding organizations to a more robust standard[14] that focusses on integrity as the force that drives the organization. It involves developing an *integrity strategy* that is characterized by a conception of ethics as a driving force of an enterprise. Ethical values shape the search for opportunities, the design of organizational systems, and the decision making processes used by individuals and groups. They provide a common frame of reference and serve as a unifying force across different functions, lines of business, and employee groups. *Organizational ethics* helps define what a company is and what it stands for.[15] An ethical corporate culture can and should also help a corporation ensure that its values and objectives are aligned with the interests of its key stakeholders. This can facilitate and enhance the organization's control systems and quality control processes to the benefit of directors, executives, shareholders, and other stakeholders.

Corporations are increasingly recognizing that sustained success in the marketplace and thus their long-term viability is very much dependent on their having continuing support from key stakeholders such as customers, employees, suppliers, and host communities. Good governance, dedicated to optimally achieving strategic objectives on a sustained basis, depends upon a culture of integrity to manage risks, maintain the support of key stakeholders, and maximize and sustain profits.

Moreover, the fact, as explained in Appendix B, that legislators and regulators are moving further into the business ethics field should not lead to complacency or a belief following the rules is enough to stay out of trouble. Far from it. Regulations tend to focus on form, sometimes at the expense of substance. Governance processes and internal control structures will work well only if those responsible for implementing them act in an ethical man-

---

14. Paine, Lynn Sharp, "Managing for Organizational Integrity," Harvard Business Review, Harvard Business School, March–April, 1994, 111. This article is reproduced beginning on page xx.
15. Ibid. 111.

ner. When it comes to audit committees, for example, it appears that Enron had all the right structures in place. Indeed, some have said the audit committee's mandate was exemplary. However, the process failed because the people who were involved were not as diligent as they should have been. Diligence in matters ethical is a business imperative, whether there are rules or not.

Readings *located at the end of the book*

Jim Goodfellow and Allan Willis, "CEO Challenge," *Camagazine* 40:1 (2007): 35–42.

Law Case Summary: Caremark National Inc.

Lynn Sharp Paine, "Managing for Organizational Integrity," *Harvard Business Review* (1994) March–April: 106–117.

	Checklist – Creating & Implementing an Ethical Corporate Culture
	An Ethical Culture: Elements & Motivation
✓	Do your organization's members share a common set of:
	• Beliefs
	• Values
	• Practices
	Is that common set of beliefs, values and practices supported by:
	• Specific identification & communications
	• Codes, guidelines & reinforcement
	• Monitoring, rewards & punishment
	Does your management team understand:
	• The elements of an ethical culture
	• The reinforcers of an ethical culture
	• Possible individual & team outcomes
	• Possible areas of improved effectiveness
	At what level does your company understand that ethical treatment is about how the interests of stakeholders are respected:
	• Board of Directors
	• Executives
	• Managers
	• Workers

	Does your ethical culture factor the need for stakeholder support into:
	• Strategic planning
	• Decision making
	Do your Board, executives, managers, and workers understand that an ethical culture:
	• Is good business
	• Enhances trust & reputation
	• Increasing numbers of companies are giving attention to it
	• Is a new benchmark expectation for:
	o Profit
	o Corporate citizenship & corporate social responsibility
	o Awards
	• Preventing surprises
	• Mitigates personal liability
	• Requires diligent risk management
	• Satisfies and encourages altruists

Developing an Ethical Corporate Culture

Chapter 3
Foundation – Leadership, Core Values & Important Issues

Key Steps

As indicated in Chapter 2, an organization's culture is the set of beliefs, norms and practices that are shared by the organization's members[1]. This culture needs to be ethical – a culture of integrity – to ensure the continuing support of shareholder and other stakeholder groups that, in turn, is so necessary for a corporation to achieve its strategic objectives on a sustained basis. In the end, a properly thought-out organizational culture – an ethical culture – provides a framework that motivates and guides appropriate employee decisions and actions in accord with the organization's strategic goals. The major steps involved are pictured in Figure 3.1.

Creating an Ethical Governance and Leadership Framework

Strong leadership is absolutely necessary in the creation of an ethical corporate culture, as is strong support by senior leaders in the organization. For many organizations establishing an ethical culture is frontier territory compared to normal business functions and the changes involved may challenge existing ways of thinking, making decisions, and getting things done. To overcome inertia or contrary momentum, to wrest turf away from those with a vested interest in the *status quo,* and to create an effective sustainable culture, will require the identification and commitment of skilled and determined leaders supported by top management and resourced ade-

---

1. Susan Key, "Organizational Ethical Culture: Real or Imagined?" Journal of Business Ethics 20 (1999): 217–218.

Figure 3.1
Creating & Implementing an Ethical Corporate Culture

quately. These lessons have been learned in the development of health and safety programs, environmental programs, and sustainability programs. Without the spark, guidance, and encouragement of strong leadership, developing an effective culture of integrity is not possible.

Leaders do not operate effectively unless their initiatives are in harmony with and supported by other aspects of a corporation's intended activities. In a modern corporation, all activities should be in support of a strategic plan that lays out strategic goals and related operational objectives. The organization's board of directors is expected to set and/or approve this strategic plan and related objectives, and to monitor its progress. The appointment of supportive executives and leaders who provide the right "tone at the top" is an essential element of the governance process, as is the oversight of appropriate processes for the establishment, launch, and maintenance of an ethical culture, including the provision of needed resources.

Leaving a vacuum instead of providing cogent guidance for employee behaviour leaves the organization open to the risks of trial and error as employees make their inevitable mistakes. Because leaving employee actions to happenstance is not acceptable risk management practice in today's world, research[2] has been conducted into how to make the most effective impact on employee actions. It has become apparent that the best approach is to provide guidance on the values that underpin the organization's strategic objectives, coupled with the strong support of top management for those values. It turns out that values are a vital element of an organizational culture because they can define important behavioural principles, and therefore guide how employees will act with the organization's stakeholders. Consequently, ethical values need to be the focus of the first part of the establishment process.

Once the core values of the organization are established, their integration into strategic and operational goals would be next in the sequence. The need for consistency between organizational goals and behaviour is essential to avoid confusion in the minds of employees and performance that conflicts with desired objectives.

After the strategic and operational parameters are in place, establishing a culture of integrity depends upon communicating organizational values and objectives effectively, and upon making employees aware of them and willing to buy into, support and follow the recommended behaviour by making appropriate decisions.

Lastly, reinforcement mechanisms need to be put in place to ensure that employees renew their awareness and commitment to the elements important to the organization's ethical culture.

Taken together, if executed effectively these steps will design and establish a *corporate ethics program* that will reduce a corporation's risk of unethical and illegal actions by employees and agents, and respond to the interests of the company's stakeholders. It will also provide evidence of due diligence on the part of directors and executives who are expected to ensure and oversee appropriate governance structures and processes. In the future, reputations for ethical leadership will depend upon the active development, operation and advocacy of corporate ethics programs based upon the topics discussed in this chapter.

Identifying and Motivating Leaders

Effective leadership starts at the top. The CEO must endorse the goals, personnel involved, process, funding, and the results obtained, or else the rest of the organization will only play lip service to the concept. CEO support is

---

2. See Gary R. Weaver. "Ethics Programs in Global Businesses: Culture's Role in Managing Ethics" *Journal of Business Ethics* 30: 1(2001): 3–15, and Gary R. Weaver, Linda Klebe Treviño & Philip L. Cochran, "Corporate Ethics Programs as Control Systems: Influences of Executive Commitment and Environmental Factors," *The Academy of Management Journal* 42:1 (1999): 41–57.

so critical that ensuring proper "tone at the top" became an important governance requirement for boards of directors in the mid-1990s[3]. The support of the board chair is also important, particularly in a strategic sense, but is usually less obvious to employees than that of the CEO, CFO, and other senior officers.

It is important to note that it is not enough for a senior corporate leader to silently or passively support an ethical corporate culture, and be considered an ethical leader. Recent research has shown[4] that unless a leader is seen to be vocal or tangibly in support of the ethical corporate culture employees will assume that the only meaningful guiding principle they should adhere to is to maximize profit with little regard to how that profit is earned.

The task of championing the development of an ethical corporate culture can be delegated by the CEO to a well-regarded executive who will be assisted by an ethics officer or ombudsperson with expertise in managing an ethics program. The champion will report to, and keep the CEO informed, and will work with the CEO in arriving at a supportable ethics program that informs and fits with the organization's strategic goals and risk management preferences.

The champion also needs an ethics committee to assist in the development of the important elements of the ethical corporate culture, and to assist in the selling of the program to the rest of management and other employees. Typically the ethics committee assists in the identification of the values and other elements of the ethics program, and then in the launch and early monitoring of the effectiveness of the launch and the program itself. As well, the committee members act as facilitators or cheerleaders during the introduction of the program.

The CEO in turn will keep the board chair, the board, and its governance subcommittee informed. The governance committee should receive ongoing reports from the ethics officer and receive, vet, and approve the final report on the proposed ethical corporate culture prior to its launch. The champion for the development of the ethics program would probably lead the presentation and be charged with the responsibility for launching the program. Needless to say, the CEO and possibly the chair of the board should visibly support the launch and critical elements of the program itself in order to assure management and employee buy in.

---

3. CICA Study, "Where were the Directors?" 1994
4. Linda Klebe Treviño, Laura Pincus Hartman, Michael Brown, "Moral Person and Moral Manager: How Executives Develop A Reputation for Ethical Leadership," *California Management Review* 42:4(2000): 128–142.

Figure 3.2
Establishing an Ethical Corporate Culture –
The Leadership Component

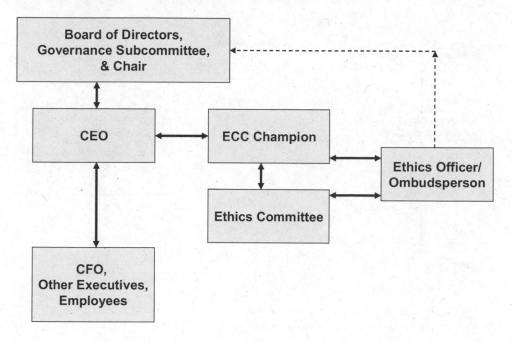

Developing the Core Values & Issues Component of an Ethical Culture

Central to the creation of an ethical corporate culture is the identification of the core values on which it is based. A comprehensive approach to this involves an analysis of stakeholder interests utilizing key frameworks for building reputation and developing core values, norms, and ethical decision criteria; as well as techniques for conducting ethics audits and ethics risk assessments. These are shown in Figure 3.3 and are discussed below.

Identifying Core Values – The Basis for Cultural Guidance

Some corporations have a good sense of what they want to achieve, the image they want to project, and what is important to their success. Most companies, however, would benefit from an orderly examination of their goals, strategies, and processes to ensure that they fit well into an effective guidance mechanism. Such an examination would benefit from considering current thinking on the following points:

Figure 3.3
Establishing an Ethical Corporate Culture –
The Core Values & Issues Component

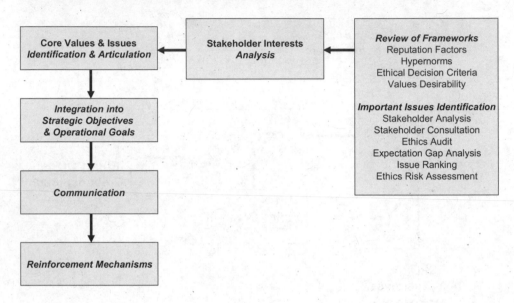

- The importance of stakeholders and their interests, and on the values they hold most dear
- The key elements underlying reputation
- The making of ethical decisions
- Problems and their management as discovered in an ethics audit and ethics risk assessment

Although it is not immediately apparent, much of this examination is focussed on identification of the key or "right" drivers of behaviour that are to be provided as guidance for employees whose actions are responsible for success and for avoiding trouble. Interestingly, it will become clear that there is a set of common drivers – a combination of specific and universal values that earn respect – that coalesce from the different examination perspectives and approaches. The identification of these universal values can be facilitated by reviewing the frameworks that have been developed to provide an understanding of reputation and of a universal set of values that bring respect in most societies.

Figure 3.4
What makes a good reputaton?

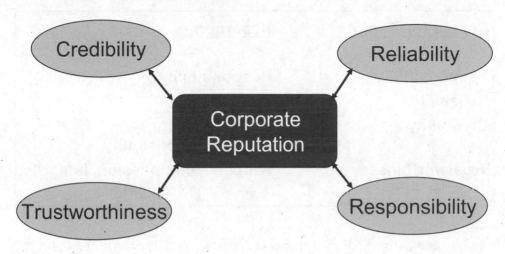

Charles J. Fombrun, *Reputation: Realizing Value from the Corporate Image* (Harvard Business School Press, 1996), *72.*

Reputational Values

Modern corporations are justifiably concerned about their reputation or image because it can attract or repel customers, employees, and other stakeholders important to their success. In this regard, many companies make significant efforts to craft, project, and monitor their image as a good corporate citizen. Charles Fombrun[5] has developed a model (see Figure 3.4) that is most useful in understanding the factors that determine corporate reputation. The four factors identified – trustworthiness, credibility, reliability and responsibility – work on a personal as well as a corporate level. For instance, they would be useful criteria for selecting a partner in life or in a professional firm. *There may be additional desirable criteria or value added, but the four identified by Fombrun can be regarded as a basic or core set of reputational values.*

Hypernorms – almost Universally Respected Values

Researchers have also been endeavouring to discover the values that are

---

5. Charles J. Fombrun, *Reputation: Realizing Value from the Corporate Image* (Harvard Business School Press, 1996).

Figure 3.5
Hypernorms Support Reputational Factors

Reputation Factors	Hypernorms
Responsibility	Responsibility
Reliability	Predictability
Credibility	Honesty, integrity, responsibility
Trustworthiness	Fairness, compassion, integrity, responsibility

most universally respected by people from different cultures around the world, since these would provide excellent touchstones for the development of an ethical culture for enterprises doing business globally. So far, the six most uniformly respected values known as *hypernorms* – are identified[6] as *honesty, fairness, compassion, integrity, predictability, and responsibility.*

Predictably, as reflected in Figure 3.5, strong hypernorms provide the basis for strong reputational factors or values. Consequently, the combined set of factors and values is worthy of adoption by an organization bent on establishing an ethical culture. Embedding the relationship between hypernorms and ethical reputation in the guidance underlying the ethical culture would be useful in establishing an understanding of the linkage in the minds of employees.

AACSB Recommended Ethical Decision Making Approaches and Criteria

Hypernorm values and reputational factors are also present in the approaches and criteria recommended by the Association to Advance Collegiate Schools of Business (AACSB)[7], the worldwide accreditation body for business schools, to be taught to business students on ethical decision

---

6. R.E. Berenbeim, The Conference Board, Director, Working Group on Global Business Ethics Principles, 1999.
7. AACSB EETF Report, 2004, Report of the Ethics Education Task Force: Ethics Education in Business Schools, Association to Advance Collegiate Schools of Business, see http://www.aacsb.edu.

Figure 3.6
Ethical Decision-making Approaches and Criteria

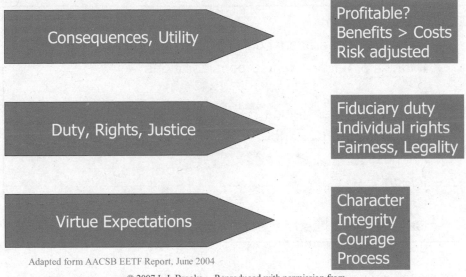

Adapted form AACSB EETF Report, June 2004

© 2007 L.J. Brooks.   Reproduced with permission from
Business & Professional Ethics for Directors, Executives & Accountants, Thomson South-Western

making as shown in Figure 3.6. The AACSB's Ethics Education Committee recommends consideration of three approaches that have their roots in earlier philosophical thinking: utilitarianism or its subset consequentialism, deontology, and virtue ethics. Leaving more detailed explanations until Chapter 8, these approaches examine the utility or consequences of a decision for the affected stakeholders, its impact on stakeholder rights, and how it corresponds to or demonstrates the virtues expected by stakeholders.

Value Desirability Framework

In terms of the decision to choose a partner that was noted above, these three approaches: Reputational, Hypernorm, and AACSB Ethical Decision Making, can be combined into a *Value Desirability Framework* that involves the two dimensions noted in Figure 3.7 – specific value added and behavioural values. To develop the full set of organizational values to underpin the ethical culture the interests of each of the organization's stakeholder groups should be examined, asking what specific value added and what behavioural factors or values are desired or expected.

Since one of the most common faults of corporate decision makers is to

Figure 3.7
Value Desirability Framework Incorporating
Reputation FActors, Hypernorms, & Ethical Decision Criteria

Specific Value-added
- Tangible or operational utility or consequences
- Intrinsic or future-oriented considerations

Behavioural Factors or Values
- Respect for others rights
- Fairness
- Integrity
- Courage
- Other value-related aspects of character.

ignore some groups of stakeholders, including the media, that may later become very important to the achievement of the corporation's strategic objectives, it is advisable that all stakeholders and their interests be included in this review. It is important to bear in mind that stakeholders judged insignificant may and often do develop media-worthy issues, or ally themselves with stronger stakeholders, so that their interests become significant in the future[8].

Figure 3.8 presents a set of values that result from a typical analysis of a company's stakeholders' interests. Shareholders, for example, are interested in profit or some other form of value added such as competitive advantage, or reputation, or image, or control of assets or process that will produce profits in the future. In addition, they are interested in values and strategies that will support and sustain future activities, in addition to protecting their rights in terms of fair, complete, and transparent disclosure and distribution of profit earned. A similar analysis of interests, undertaken for other stakeholders, would likely identify the values listed below. The elements of the reputational, hypernorms, and ethical decision criteria are provided for reference. When reviewed as a whole, these stakeholder analyses fit well with the Value Desirability Framework involving stakeholder specific tangible and intangible value added plus behavioural values.

---

8. For a more detailed discussion of this stakeholder impact dynamic, refer to Chapter 8.

Figure 3.8
Identifying Values for an Ethical Corporate Culture

Sources of Values	Tangible or Operational, Intrinsic & Behavioural Values
Stakeholder Interests	Shareholders
	Tangible/Operational - Value Added, Net Profit,
	Intangible - Competitive Advantage, Image, Reputation
	Behavioural - Honesty (**H**), Integrity (**I**), Fairness (**F**), Credibility (**Cred**),
	Reliability/Predictability (**R/P**), Responsibility (**R**)
	Consumer
	Tangible/Operational - Value in use
	Intrinsic Value - Innovativeness, Environmental Friendliness, ...
	Behavioural - **H, I, F**, Compassion (**C**), **R/P, R**
	Employee - Fair Pay & Opportunity
	- Ethical Reputation, ...
	- **H, I, F, C, R/P, R**
	Environmentalists - Sustainability, **H, I, F, C, R/P, R**
	Community – Support, **H, I, F, C, R/P, R**
	Other – ....
Reputation Factors	Trustworthiness, **Cred**ibility, **R**eliability, **R**esponsibility
Hypernorms – key values in most cultures/societies	**H**onesty, **F**airness, **C**ompassion, **I**ntegrity, **P**redictability, **R**esponsibility
Ethical Decision Criteria See Chapter 8	*Net Positive Utility or Consequences* from an action Net profit, Net Cost-Benefit Analysis, Net Risk-Benefit Analysis *Observance of Duties, Rights and/or Fairness* *Fulfillment of Virtues Expected*

In summary, in order to develop a set of core values to build into its ethics program, a corporation should analyse the interests of its stakeholders using a framework similar to the above and referring to known reputation factors, hypernorms, ethical decision criteria, and a values desirability framework.

Identifying Important Ethical Issues for Cultural Guidance

During the stakeholder values analysis, the corporation should be alert to specific issues that are of concern so that these can be adequately addressed in the ethical guidance given to employees. Often an issue, such as environmental sensitivity, can be covered by a general principle that flows from a specific set of values, but occasionally specific treatment is necessary to avoid confusion or provide the best signal to all stakeholders that this is a matter of high priority or risk and its treatment or specific aspects of it are to be handled in a certain way.

In addition to a review of stakeholder interests and values, important issues can be identified from scans of industry and other company guidance documents such as mission statements, codes of conduct, and so on. Electronic summaries of codes and code content are available on several websites that are referenced on the EthicsCentre website at http://www. ethicscentre.ca. Articles on the development of codes are also noted.

To make sure important issues are not overlooked, corporations can hire consultants to undertake environmental scans of the news media and provide up-to-date advice on issues of concern, or their own personnel can undertake these reviews. If the scans are done internally, corporations would be well-advised to seek expert advice on which issues are likely to emerge as significant risks, and how other companies are dealing with them.

Some companies convene *stakeholder consultation groups* in an effort to stay in touch with their constituents and their interests. These groups can be useful, as well, in testing reactions to past events and proposed solutions. They create a bond that can be helpful in working through problems that arise on an ongoing basis. Recognizing the importance of stakeholder consultation groups, the Canadian Standards Association (CSA) has developed a protocol for their formation and engagement[9].

Some corporations engage in *ethics audits* as a means to identify and understand ethical issues affecting their strategies or activities, to ensure they are managed effectively from a risk perspective. An ethics audit involves reviewing all or part of an operation – its personnel, complaints by customers and suppliers; environmental and health and safety reports; quality standards and similar documents – in order to discover what the important issues are and might be. Sometimes such audits are done by outside consultants, sometimes by a squad of promising junior executives from another part of the enterprise, or by the company's internal auditors. The audit report could be part of the ongoing ethics program and forwarded to the ethics officer, chief risk officer, the CEO and relevant board subcommittee. The best known of these was the Dow Corning ethics audit[10] that unfortunately failed to raise the problems associated with the company's leaking silicone breast implants that ultimately were responsible for putting the company into bankruptcy. Even so, Dow Corning's CEO applauded its ethics audit process for the earlier successes it had brought. With proper guidance and understanding of audit and interview techniques, the ethics audit can be a very effective mechanism for ethics issues identification and assessment.

---

9. Canadian Standards Association, *A Guide to Public Involvement* (Z764), 1996.
10. See the "Dow Corning Ethics Audit Case" in Leonard J. Brooks, *Business & Professional Ethics for Directors, Executives & Accountants*, 4e, (Thomson South-Western, 2007), 208–9.

A logical output of the process of ethics issues identification and articulation is an understanding of which issues pose significant risks for the organization. Two further techniques can be used to identify and then rank the importance of the ethics risks involved. As part of the issues identification process, examiners can use *expectation gap analysis*, assessing the difference between what stakeholders expect and what the company is delivering to identify *ethics risks*[11], and then classify their nature and their significance.

Salience research by Mitchell, Agle and Wood[12] suggests that ethics issues can be classified into those dealing with:

- Legitimate claims from stakeholders – those protected by law or sanctioned by ethical norms
- Claims from powerful stakeholders – who have the power to influence the achievement of the corporation's objectives
- Urgent claims – often from victims or soon-to-be victims

Importantly, the urgent claims are usually the most significant because of their ability to influence the media, who in turn influence the public and/or powerful politicians who have the power to regulate or influence corporate behaviour. The Mitchell, Agle and Wood Salience Model is reproduced in Figure 3.9. Care must be taken to remember the dynamic nature of the salience classification[13] when projecting developments in the future.

Figure 3.10 represents the ethics issue and risk identification and ranking approach as a three phase exercise, and brings together several of the tasks suggested to date.

At the conclusion of the search for important ethical issues facing a corporation, a list of specific topics requiring treatment might emerge such as shown in Figure 3.11.

---

11. An ethics risk exists where stakeholder expectations are not met.
12. R.K Mitchell,., B.R., Agle, & D.J., Wood, "Toward a Theory of Stakeholder Identification and Salience: Defining the Principle of Who and What Really Counts," *Academy of Management Review* 22(1997): 853–886.
13. T. Rowley, "Moving Beyond Dyadic Ties: A network Theory of Stakeholder Influences," *Academy of Management Review* 22(1997): 887–910.

Figure 3.9
Stakeholder Interest/claim Classification – Salience

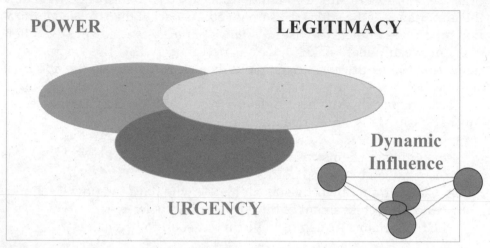

R.K Mitchell,., B.R., Agle, & D.J., Wood, "Toward a Theory of Stakeholder Identification and Salience: Defining the Principle of Who and What Really Counts," Academy of Management Review 22(1997): 853-886.
T. Rowley, "Moving Beyond Dyadic Ties: A network Theory of Stakeholder Influences", Academy of Management Review 22(1997): 887-910.

Figure 3.10
Ethics Risk & Opportunity Identification & Assessment

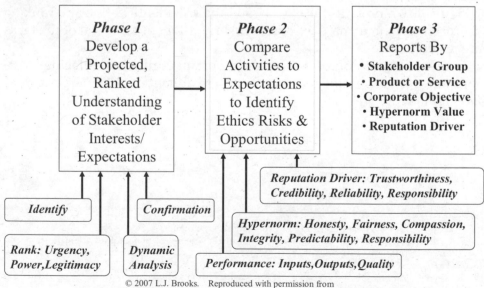

© 2007 L.J. Brooks.   Reproduced with permission from
Business & Professional Ethics for Directors, Executives & Accountants, Thomson South-Western

Figure 3.11
Examples of Specific Topics Requiring Treatment
in an Ethical Corporate Culture

Corporate values & related guidance
- Identification and rationale linked to mission, reputation & strategy
- Responsibility for endorsement, commitment & accountability by CEO & all others
- Responsibility for compliance, consultation & whistle-blowing
- Importance of character, integrity & courage

Stakeholder interests and expectations
- Fair treatment of customers & employees – pay, discrimination, complaints, etc.
- Respect for the environment for direct & indirect impacts, stewardship & sustainability
- Respect for the health of employees, customers & others influenced
- Conflicts of interest with shareholders
- Bribery and other unethical behaviour
- Respect for the law & for other cultures

Corporate citizenship
- Definition in terms of values, mission and activities
- External leadership objective

Processes endorsed
- Measurement of impacts – Global Reporting Initiative & AccountAbility frameworks
- Ethical decision making criteria & process
- Ethics inquiry & whistle-blower protection programs
- Ethical risk management
- Ethical crisis management
- Designation of an ethics champion & of an annual reporting & review process

	Checklist – Creating & Implementing an Ethical Corporate Culture	
	Leadership, Core Values & Important Issues	
✓	Create a Governance & Leadership Framework	
	• Clarify roles of board & governance/ethics subcommittee, chair, CEO	
	• Identify ethics champion, chief ethics officer & role of each	
	• Identify reporting relationships & expectations	
	• Identify responsibilities and performance expectations	
	Develop the Core Values & Issues Foundation	
	Develop Core Value set by considering:	
	• Reputational values – *trustworthiness, credibility, reliability, responsibility*	
	• Hypernorms – *honesty, fairness, compassion, integrity, predictability, and responsibility.*	
	• Ethical decision making criteria – stakeholder impact analysis	

	• Constructing a Values Desirability Framework
Identify important issues requiring cultural guidance by:	
	• Stakeholder Impact Analysis
	• Environmental scanning
	• Stakeholder consultation
	• Ethics audit
	• Expectations gap assessment
	• Ranking issues – *urgent claims before powerful and legal*
	• Ranking issues – ethics risk assessment

Developing an Ethical Corporate Culture

Chapter 4
Guidance Communications –
Mission Statement, Code of Conduct, Decision Aids

In addition to the proper integration of the desired values into operational goals, implementing an ethical culture will require appropriate communication of values and initiation of reinforcement mechanisms.

Integration of Core Values into Strategic Objectives and Operational Goals

Strategic objectives should be set to optimize the corporation's potential to encourage the support of its key stakeholder groups because this support will determine the success of the organization in the future. The final set of objectives will certainly involve trade-offs between owners, management, customers, and other groups, so ignoring the interests and related core values of one or more of the stakeholder groups would be short-sighted. Consequently, whatever strategic objectives are adopted should be compared with and adjusted to reflect the set of core interests and values developed in the stakeholder analysis described above.

It may be more efficient to create a corporation's strategic objectives to reflect the findings of the stakeholder analysis in the first instance. For example, the findings of the Values Desirability Analysis (see Figures 3.7 and 3.8) should identify the tangible and intrinsic interests, and behavioural values desired by each stakeholder group. When combined with a vision of the future and an assessment of the resources of the organization, these findings should provide a guide to desired competitive advantages, values and desired behavioural principles. For example, if a substantial segment of customers want fuel-efficient cars because they value and want to protect the environment, it would be highly risky to develop a vision and competitive advantage based upon high-powered, gas-guzzling vehicles.

Operational goals should flow from, and be compatible with, ethical strategic objectives to avoid confusion and mistakes. For example, if customers value honesty, integrity and transparency, it would be wise to craft strategic objectives and operational objectives that signal their importance to the corporation's employees. In the case of General Motors' Saturn Division, this led to the establishment of "no haggle pricing" which found high appreciation from women who preferred to deal with credible dealers. On the other hand, Sears automotive repair shops operationalized their drive for profits by establishing a bonus scheme for service managers that, when coupled with an aggressive, insufficiently ethical culture, induced and allowed the managers to benefit from selling unneeded services to unsuspecting customers. Given the relatively immediate sharing of information via the internet, such as Intel's decision not to recall a flawed math co-processor on their early Pentium 4 chip, the damage to corporate reputation from unethical strategic objectives and operational goals can be swift and serious. Ethical core values need to be included in both from the start.

Effective Communication of Values

A mission statement and code of ethics or conduct are viewed by most companies as essential first steps in developing and communicating the values of an organization. On their own, however, they cannot result in the development of an ethical corporate culture.

A mission statement is a short, inspiring, visionary communication to employees and other stakeholders concerning the purpose, values, and objectives of an organization, and what is expected from employees in terms of promoting such values and objectives. The existence of a strong set of widely understood and generally accepted values has been cited as a reason why Johnson & Johnson was able to handle its crisis with the poisoned Tylenol tablets so effectively. A company that does not have a firm set of accepted values will be at a greater risk of the occurrence of unethical acts, and if a crisis occurs, may have to create these values "on the fly" in the middle of it. Such a company will find it very difficult to develop a solution that is well thought out and consistent with its longer-term objectives, and may end up making matters worse. Situations where absence of sound values has allowed poor practices in day-to-day operations or in crisis situations include:

- Firestone Tires on the Ford Explorer

Figure 4.1
Johnson & Johnson Credo

We believe our first responsibility is to the doctors, nurses, and patients, to mothers and all others who use our products and services. In meeting their needs everything we do must be of high quality. We must constantly strive to reduce our costs in order to maintain reasonable prices. Customers' orders must be serviced promptly and accurately. Our suppliers and distributors must have an opportunity to make a fair profit.

We are responsible to our employees, the men and women who work with us throughout the world. Everyone must be considered as an individual. We must respect their dignity and recognize their merit. They must have a sense of security in their jobs. Compensation must be fair and adequate and working conditions clean, orderly, and safe. Employees must feel free to make suggestions and complaints. There must be equal opportunity for employment, development and advancement for those qualified. We must provide competent management, and their actions must be just and ethical.

We are responsible to the communities in which we live and work and to the world community as well. We must be good citizens – support good works and charities and bear our fair share of taxes. We must encourage civic improvements and better health and education. We must maintain in good order the property we are privileged to use, protecting the environment and natural resources.

Our final responsibility is to our stockholders. Business must make a sound profit. We must experiment with new ideas. Research must be carried on, innovative programs developed and mistakes paid for. New equipment must be purchased, new facilities provided, and new products launched. Reserved must be created to provide for adverse times. When we operate according to these principles, the stockholders should realize a fair return.

- Product recalls were initially denied to reduce legal liability, but which signaled a lack of concern over customer safety and resulted in a loss of additional sales, and higher legal costs.
- Dow Corning Silicone Breast Implants – Dow Corning executives resisted product recalls and adequate restitution even though they knew silicone leakage was likely and thousands of women were reporting similar illnesses. The entire company was ultimately put into receivership by the legal settlement.

For reference, Johnson & Johnson's Mission Statement is reproduced below.

A code of conduct or ethics is usually a much longer document than the mission statement that covers the same purpose, values, and objectives in somewhat greater depth, and usually goes on to propose principles and rules of conduct. It provides general and specific guidance as well as rationale for expected behaviour.

At the extreme, a mission statement can be a focus-providing document of only one page, whereas a code of conduct is frequently published in booklet form of twenty or more pages. A company's mission statement is usually featured on its public website, and a code of conduct is usually available via the company's internal website. Both mission statements and codes of ethics or conduct can and should be used on an ongoing basis as a means of communicating an organization's values and objectives, and as a means of measuring and monitoring performance designed to achieve those objectives.

The development and implementation of a process to articulate values and to develop a mission statement and/or code is often delegated to one department in an organization. It is essential that, however, managers at all levels of the organization, including top management, support the need to develop an ethical corporate culture and that they are involved in the process. To be successful a mission statement or code should:

- Articulate the organization's strategically determined core reason for being and goals
- Reflect/articulate values, issues, and responsibilities to stakeholders that are important to success, to the type of corporate citizen it wishes to be, and that ought to be shared throughout the organization
- Involve grassroots/front line buy in throughout its development
- Take the outside world into account by determining where the organization can make a difference (mission) and by considering the real pressures under which the individual must make decisions (code)

Once the issues to be raised and values to be signalled are identified, an orientation should be chosen for the mission statement or code of conduct. This choice is now understood to be an important contributor to the overall effectiveness of the code of conduct because the orientation of the code determines the degree of employee buy in to the values it articulates. The choices of orientation noted by Treviño and her colleagues[1] are:

- An integrity, or values-based orientation
- A compliance-based orientation
- An orientation designed for the satisfaction of external stakeholders

---

1. Linda Klebe Treviño, Gary R. Weaver, David G. Gibson, and Barbara Ley Toffler, "Managing Ethics and Legal Compliance: What Works and What Hurts," *California Management Review* 41 (1999): 135–139.

- An orientation designed in order to protect top management from blame
- A combination of the above approaches

The Treviño research has shown that codes of conduct, and ethics programs, based upon integrity or shared values are more likely to be effective than those based on compliance-oriented rules, protection for the top management or just satisfaction of external stakeholders. The most effective orientation, however, appears to be a combination approach in which shared values represent the dominant orientation, and compliance concerns are secondary. It is to be hoped that codes of conduct gravitate toward this values-dominated, combination approach[2].

It should be noted that Lynn Sharp Paine believes that, "there is no one right integrity strategy. Factors such as management personality, company history, culture, lines of business, and industry regulations must be taken into account when shaping an appropriate set of values and designing an implementation program."[3] She describes the key features to developing a strategy reinforcing integrity within an organization by referring to efforts made by organizations that have achieved success in this area.

Ms. Paine goes on to say that, "success in creating a climate for responsible and ethically sound behaviour requires continuing effort and a considerable investment of time and resources. A glossy code of conduct, a high-ranking ethics officer, a training program, an annual ethics audit – these trappings of an ethics program do not necessarily add up to a responsible, law-abiding organization whose espoused values match its actions. A formal ethics program can serve as a catalyst and a support system, but organizational integrity depends on the integration of the company's values into its driving systems."[4]

---

2. Note that according to a 1999 Conference Board Report, the values orientation is only one of four they have identified, but it is the only one to be, "found in every region and is the dominant form in Europe." The four orientations that the Conference Board used are:
   - Instrumental – adherence is essential to success
   - Compliance – statement of do's and don'ts
   - Stakeholder Commitment – acknowledgment of company accountability to various constituencies
   - Values – declaration that certain ethics principles are essential to what it means to be an employee of the company
   US companies are said to, "rely most often on the instrumental justification," whereas, "Canadian, Japanese, and Latin American companies are more evenly divided among the four different categories." Ronald E. Berenbeim, *Global Corporate Ethics Practice: A Developing Consensus*, (New York: The Conference Board, Inc, 1999): 8.
3. Lynn Sharp Paine, "Managing for Organizational Integrity," *Harvard Business Review*, March – April (1994): 112. Reprinted as a reading at the end of the book.
4. Ibid., page 112.

Input from all Levels

The drafting of the code should be done keeping in mind the need to use plain language that can be understood by all readers. When the steering committee is comfortable with the draft, the chairman and CEO should read it to make sure they are willing to provide strong support.

After the draft code is blessed by the chairman and CEO, it should be taken to representative groups of employees for their reactions and suggestions for improvement in clarity, coverage, and sensitivity to local issues. These sessions can be useful for pre-training the corporation's trainers, and in gaining early understanding and commitment from informal leaders at all levels within the corporation. This can be particularly helpful when launching the code, and in its early interpretation.

It may be helpful for the steering group to start with stakeholder, particularly employee, input prior to arriving at a first draft. The objective in this approach is to obtain employee input before major decisions are made, or even floated as ideas, rather than subsequently, as feedback. This is difficult to organize and achieve, but avoids the problem of negative feedback on a steering committee draft being inevitably seen by senior management as a criticism of the draft. It may also inhibit the flow of ideas from employees. Preliminary input may, for example, be obtained from small, facilitated groups of employees specifically selected to provide representation from various ranks, levels, departments, cultures, and genders.

Feedback Sessions and Gap Analysis

One helpful framework for feedback sessions involves sending out the draft code to be read in advance. When the session participants convene, the can be asked to debate the following questions:

- What did you expect to find in the code? What was missing?
- Was any aspect of the code unclear?
- Are there any barriers to the introduction and use of the code?

The answers to these questions will facilitate a gap analysis that will permit the improvement of the code, its acceptance, and adherence to it. The final version of the code should be approved by the board of directors upon the favourable recommendation of the company's senior officers, all of whom must actively endorse it, and encourage its subsequent use.

Decision Aids

In addition to the organization's mission statement and code of conduct, other helpful aids are often produced to remind employees what they should consider when considering a decision or action. IBM, for example, first produced a pocket-size guide and later an online version for ease of reference. The intention is to ensure the organization and its employees are in a defensible position legally and ethically.

Decision aids should include, in abbreviated form, the ethical values and major issues that employees should bear in mind. This might be arranged to cover the AACSB's approaches, or a set of sniff tests and additional questions that cover the impacts on stakeholder interests. These are explored more fully in Chapter 8.

Organizational policy should hold employees responsible for using the decision aids provided, and if a potentially unethical decision is identified, the employee is responsible for consulting a manager with training in applying such analysis, or a designated person such as the company's chief ethics officer[5].

Even if an organization does not have a quick reference decision aid, employees should have an understanding of ethical decision making and know where and when to seek guidance. Ethical decision-making criteria need to be a formal part of an organization's ethical culture.

Checklist – Creating & Implementing an Ethical Corporate Culture		
Guidance Communications – **Mission Statement, Code of Conduct, Decision Aids**		
✓	Guidance communications should be based on core values & important issues that are integrated into :	
	• Strategic goals	
	• Operational goals	

---

5. A chief ethics officer is charged with the overall responsibility for the ethics program for a company. Another title could be chief ethics & compliance officer. Additional details are available from the Ethics & Compliance Officer Association at http://www.theecoa.org

	Effective guidance communications should include:
	• Mission Statement
	o Short, inspiring, focussed on key values
	• Code of Conduct
	o Incorporate core values
	o Cover important issues needing guidance
	o Choose orientation – integrity or values-based vs. compliance-based, or combination approach
	o Use input from all levels
	o Use feedback sessions and gap analysis
	• Decision Aids
	o Online or not?
	o Usage requirement
	o Sniff tests
	o Consultation required if problematic
	o Key ethical decision criteria
	o Reporting requirement

Developing an Ethical Corporate Culture

Chapter 5
Developing Commitment & Understanding – Launch

Training Program

An effective ethics-training program should cover all employees within an organization. It should also be provided to agents and to providers of out-sourced services. It should complement the launching of the mission statement or code, and should be designed to help employees and agents:

- Understand the relevance of the mission statement or code and the values it puts forward to the organization's competitive advantage and strategy
- Understand the mission statement, ethical values, and principles of the organization
- Recognize, analyze, and resolve ethical issues in their own jobs
- Know what support resources are available to them if they have questions or are faced with situations involving ethical dilemmas
- Provide feedback on current ethics issues, ethics performance and the training program

Ethics Workshops

Ethics workshops provide one way of training employees. The main advantage of holding workshops is that they enable employees to work together in small groups and to thus learn by doing.

The workshops should be structured so that they involve employees from a single, small work group or employees from a small number of related work groups. This will allow the employees at the workshop to focus on issues relevant to their workplace. The workshop should be led by the manager or supervisor to whom the group(s) report(s), thus reinforcing management's commitment to and responsibility for ethics. It is important however, if the manager is to participate directly as a presenter, that he or she has had prior training and has demonstrated commitment to the mission and code and to the values that underlie them. If this is not established in advance, it is better that the manager be part of the audience rather than at the podium. In any event, it is often beneficial to provide a facilitator to the group. The facilitator could be an ethics advisor, a consultant, or an individual working in human resources, the comptroller's department or the internal audit department.

Workshop Agenda

The workshop agenda should allow for open, informal, two-way communications as well as a formal presentation. An appropriate way to achieve this is to have small group discussions of challenging issues or case studies, which are relevant to the particular group and its work. The scheduled time for each should be a minimum of one to one and an half hours, with flexibility for more time if the discussion of issues is rewarding. If the group holding the workshop has regularly scheduled meetings, ethics workshops could be held as one of them. Whenever possible, the CEO should make a personal appearance during the launch. In very large organizations this will likely be impossible. In this case, he or she should send a message by video and make a personal appearance at selected workshops, especially those for executive and senior management personnel.

A suggested workshop agenda is outlined below, with some supplementary tips added:

- Introduction
- Ethics program overview
- Mission statement review
- Video (include excerpts from code of ethics and presentation by senior management)
- Code of ethics content review
- Decision aids and frameworks for problems to be faced (see Chapter 8)
- Ethics resources and process (available for guidance and support)
- Group discussion of issues raised in the code, or in the workplace and case studies from the group's workplace showing how the code should be used as a reference tool

- Questionnaire (to provide anonymous feedback on ethics issues, completeness of coverage of the code, performance, and training program)
- Compliance sign off (participants should be asked to sign a card agreeing to comply with the organization's ethics policy)

Workshop support

There are a number of generic support materials available in the marketplace for workshop leaders that can be accessed by the organization or the facilitator. A partial list of these is available from the Canadian Centre for Ethics & Corporate Policy[1].

Workshop leaders would likely benefit from a training session which would review the materials available prior to the choice of specific materials for the group they are to lead. In workshops for leaders, the following issues might be considered:

- The letter to employees from the workshop leader inviting them to attend the workshop. The letter should request employees to reread material presented to them during the launch of the mission statement or code, such as the letter from the CEO, the mission statement, and the code of ethics. Frequently, it would be prudent to provide another copy of relevant material, particularly if it is several years old. The letter could also ask employees to identify and think about ethical issues which exist in their workplace.
- Agenda, video, overheads and handouts
- List of typical ethical issues likely to arise for discussion
- Reference to one or two articles or extracts from a book. One advantage of this is that it informs employees that business ethics is a widely considered and reputable academic and practical subject, and not just a whim of their particular management.
- Questionnaires and compliance sign-off cards
- Reinforcement – newsletters
- Assignment of responsibility, measurement of effectiveness, reports and reporting lines

Follow-up

To reinforce management responsibility for ethics, the results of the train-

---

1. See the Canadian Centre for Ethics & Corporate Policy website at http://www.ethicscentre.ca

ing program should be reviewed by senior management as part of the normal management process. This should include review by a committee of the organization's Board of Directors. The facilitator would report on the questionnaire results, including new ideas for improving the training program, and ethics issues that need management attention.

Employees recruited after the training program would each receive a copy of all the material used by employees during the program. They would then have an informal review with their supervisor, discuss any matters that may be of concern, or any new issues that have come to light since the training program. The new employees would then be asked to sign a compliance statement.

	Checklist – Creating & Implementing an Ethical Corporate Culture
	Development of Commitment & Understanding – Launch
✓	Training Program/Ethics Workshop
	• Identify ongoing responsibility for development & presentation
	• Organizational leaders speak in person or by video and endorse values & ethics program (CEO, other officers)
	• Workshop leader/facilitator has training or experience
	• Coverage should include:
	○ Introduction
	○ Ethics program overview
	○ Mission statement review
	○ Video (include excerpts from code of ethics and presentation by senior management)
	○ Code of ethics content review
	○ Decision aids and frameworks (see Chapter 8) for problems to be faced
	○ Ethics resources & process (available for guidance & support)
	○ Group discussion of issues raised in the code, in the workplace, or in case studies from the group's workplace showing how the code should be used as a reference tool
	○ Questionnaire (to provide anonymous feedback on ethics issues, completeness of coverage of the code, performance, and the training program)
	○ Compliance sign off agreeing to comply with the organization's ethics policy

		• Workshop support should include:
		○ Letter to employees from the workshop leader, inviting them to attend the workshop, and to suggest they anonymously submit ethical issues for possible discussion
		○ Agenda, video, overheads and handouts
		○ List of typical ethical issues likely to arise for discussion
		○ Articles or book extracts to frame key issues
		○ Questionnaires and compliance sign off cards
		○ Reinforcement – newsletters
		○ Assignment of responsibility, measurement of effectiveness, reports, and reporting lines
		• Follow-up should include board & senior management review

Maintaining an Ethical Corporate Culture

Chapter 6
Reinforcement & Compliance

Effective Reinforcement of Values

Once a mission statement or code of ethics has been developed, its adoption and the values inherent in it must be continually reinforced and supported by all of the organization's systems and functions. The board of directors should ensure that responsibility for this is defined. It is often useful for management to appoint an ethics officer and/or form an ethics committee composed of members from senior management to direct employee training and compliance programs, and to direct communications regarding ethics.

Developing an ethical corporate culture depends upon management leadership and commitment to establish processes throughout the organization to assist all employees to understand the values of the organization and to incorporate these values in their day-to-day activities. Several aspects of organizational activity should be involved including: management communications, development and training programs, ethics workshops, job definition and reward systems, whistle-blowing systems, and the role that ethics advisors or officers can play.

Management Communications Concerning Ethical Conduct

It is absolutely essential that senior management be visibly involved in and committed to developing an understanding of the mission statement or code of ethics by all stakeholders. Ongoing management communications must emphasize support for the organization's mission statement and code of ethics, or employees will not use them. Such communications will reinforce the messages provided by management when launching the mission statement and during the ethics training programs. Ongoing management communications can take place in a number of ways:

- A visible contribution by the CEO at the beginning, possibly of booklets, pocket cards or other media, such as videos, that are used to introduce the organization's ethics policy, mission, or code.
- Letters by the CEO to senior management, all employees, suppliers, contractors, customers, and shareholders should include and introduce the mission or code, emphasize its importance, and link it to the organization's values.
- A periodic ethics reminder letter can be sent from the CEO to employees, customers and suppliers on a quarterly or semi-annual basis. The letter may, for example, include discussion of the results of past training programs, any future training plans, contemplated changes to the mission statement or code of ethics, and any current concerns or issues that need to be considered.
- The chief ethics officer[1] should present a report to the board or an appropriate subcommittee thereof such as ethics, governance, or audit on the status of the company's ethics program, any instances or patterns of conduct worthy of revised guidance or action, any trends noted in environmental scans[2] that will impact the company, and any suggested revisions to the ethics program.
- The annual report and annual meeting should include reports from the CEO and directors on how the ethics program is being managed.
- Speeches given by the CEO should include a reference to the code and ethical issues whenever appropriate.
- Employee newsletters should include discussion of relevant ethical issues.
- Company forms and reports should be modified to reflect the mission statement or code of ethics.
- A company website could be established to house the code, updates, news events, and awards for good performance.
- Communications from senior management on specific issues, particularly on strategic and tactical plans, should contain appropriate references stressing compliance with the organization's code of ethics or conduct. For example, it is most helpful when senior man-

---

1. A chief ethics officer is responsible for the ethics program for a company. For further information see the Ethics & Compliance Officer Association website at http://www.theecoa.org
2. The term environmental scan is used here to refer to scans for issues likely to affect all stakeholders, not just environmentalists.

agement comment on the values that underpin the company's reputation, and the importance of vigilance in the maintenance of those values.

Communications from the CEO can also be very effective in introducing an ethics training program. As well, CEOs frequently meet with senior management in formal meetings, both large and small, and informally. The most effective reinforcement of all is for the CEO to behave ethically and to constantly refer to ethical values in all messages he or she delivers on all subjects. There is no important subject to which ethics is irrelevant.

Reinforcement through management capability development

Discussion and consideration of ethical issues should be integrated, as much as possible, with the normal systems and processes established by management. Management could, for example, use a portion of a regular meeting to discuss policy issues and any specific matters that may need resolution. Management teams would also benefit from periodically meeting in order to do the following activities:

- Review the code of ethics and any criteria, tools, and processes that may be discussed for identifying and resolving ethical issues.
- Discuss relevant ethical issues with a view to determining whether they were handled properly, whether feedback mechanisms were effective, and whether the code needs to be revised.
- Hear from, and provide feedback to, the corporation's ethics officer on the matters noted above for reporting to the board subcommittees.

Reinforcement through an annual ethics training program

Reinforcement of the original training program is needed to ensure success. One approach that might be taken is to develop a simplified and updated refresher workshop that can be held annually. The refresher workshop would differ from the original workshop in the following ways:

- Improved by incorporating suggestions provided by employees who participated in the original workshop.
- Enhanced through introduction and discussion of cases; real if possible, but disguised, that would provide insights into current or projected problems.

- Enhanced through the discussion of ethical decision-making aids and frameworks (see Chapter 8) as they are to be applied in cases and to issues expected to be encountered.
- Updated for changes to policies, issues, and resources.
- Updated to include the status of ethics issues, and concerns raised in questionnaires prepared for prior programs.
- Simplified by eliminating the video, and by reducing the amount of time taken to formally present the program.

As in the original training program, it will be important to have senior people attend, and to report the results of the workshops and of the questionnaires submitted by participants.

Reinforcement through integration into general training

There is growing recognition of the importance of integrating the mission statement or code of ethics into an organization's general training program. This approach emphasizes the important role that ethics plays in an organization. A discussion of ethics can easily be integrated with current examples into training programs in the following areas:

- Orientation
- Supervisory/management skills
- Risk management
- Safety
- Environmental protection
- Legal issues and considerations
- Financial controls
- Internal audit

Mechanisms such as these are indicative of how pervasively an organization should look for ways to reinforce the values and other governance propositions to executives and other employees.

The board of directors itself should also be the focus of reinforcement sessions as their inability to govern according to reasonable ethical standards has been responsible for many recent financial scandals such as Enron, WorldCom, Adelphia, Tyco and Parmalat to name a few.

Some directors, executives, and managers find it difficult to appreciate why a high level of reinforcement is needed for an effective ethics program. They should keep in mind, however, that an ethics program is absolutely critical to the company's reputation, and therefore its future success.

Reinforcement through feedback

Allowing opportunities for employee feedback on ethical issues will increase employee involvement and interest in ethics. Employee feedback will also improve an organization's ability to become aware of ethical issues and to thus appropriately address them. Feedback can be facilitated in the following ways:

- Appointment of an ethics officer, or an ombudsperson
- Establishment of:
  - A subcommittee of the board of directors for general oversight
  - An ethics inquiry hotline
  - A protected whistle-blowing program designed internally or outsourced to induce the greatest level of employee trust
  - Ethics committees in all relevant units
  - Employee assistance programs in all relevant units

These facilitations must be readily available and known to employees. Any responses must be treated as confidential. It is also important for management to establish processes to appropriately handle and respond to any feedback when it is received. Failure to do so will lead to employee cynicism about the process and will thus undermine its effectiveness. Some of the key elements of effective feedback processes can be summarized as follows:

- Allocate sufficient resources to the process to permit follow-up
- Document feedback received
- Identify criteria to help establish priorities
- Establish policies concerning confidentiality
- Involve management when policies are challenged on ethical grounds
- Establish a process to provide feedback to the individual who raised the matter, and when relevant, to all employees

Reinforcement through recognition

The evaluation and promotion of individuals should be based in part on their adherence to the values of the organization. Management should also recognize and reward exemplary behaviour by individual employees or groups of employees. This will reinforce compliance with the mission statement or code of ethics. Recognition by management can take many forms. Employees can, for example, be recognized publicly in newsletters or privately in a letter from senior management.

Reinforcement through job descriptions and reward systems

Where possible the systems of the corporation should bring to the employee's mind and reinforce the need for ethical behaviour. Building the requirement for ethical action into job descriptions sends an early signal to all those who are hired. Similarly, the inclusion of ethical activity as a dimension of assessable behaviour for annual merit increases will keep ethical behaviour in focus on a continuing basis. For example, the job description of the purchasing manager might specifically include the responsibility to ensure purchasing employees are aware of, and follow the employer's values on matters such as not taking kickbacks, or staying within stated limits for gifts or favours, objective assessments of supplier value, and concern about the supplier's own sustainability or employee practices.

Illustrative Case: Kickbacks for Tires

X Ltd. was a medium-sized owner-managed company that distributed and repaired heavy construction tires. Sam, the owner, was a pillar of the community and as honest as the day is long. He was determined that his company would be run in a trustworthy and ethical manner. He had a written code of conduct that he required all employees to read. It was posted on notice boards throughout the premises. At that time, this was well ahead of common practice.

Furthermore, in the code was a specific prohibition on accepting or giving personal favours relating to the business of the company. Sam was scrupulous in this respect in all his own dealings.

Sam was absolutely mortified when he was told by his auditors that they suspected that his purchasing personnel were taking kickbacks for steering company business to particular suppliers. "It's right in the code," he said, "why did this happen?"

After an investigation by the auditors confirmed that kickbacks were in fact being taken, he asked what he could have done differently.

This case illustrates the necessity for putting the code into practice. Yes, there was a code; yes, kickbacks were prohibited. However, the code went no further than the notice board. Nowhere in the purchasing manager's job description was a responsibility for ensuring his department was conducted on an ethical basis. The annual performance appraisals of the purchasing personnel never once touched on the issue of kickbacks.

The moral of this story is to operationalise your code. Build the ethical requirements right into job descriptions, communications, and performance appraisals.

Reinforcement through Whistleblower Programs & Inquiry Services

It is very easy to undermine an ethics program by failing to provide a mechanism for inquiry or consultation. The concepts included in a code of ethics or conduct are frequently complex and unfamiliar. Employees therefore often have questions about their applicability, and need someone to consult.

Unfortunately, employees may realize that something is wrong, but are afraid to ask about it or to bring the wrongdoing to the notice of company officials. In many cultures, it is not considered appropriate to tell on someone. The consequences of doing so can involve hostility from by fellow employees, retribution from the person reported on, or from managers who are caught up in the process who may have known about the problem but took no action, or who are friends of the accused. In any of these cases the fall out for the person making the inquiry or report can be quite unpleasant, involving loss of merit, promotion, and often their jobs.

This negative reaction to doing what is right, and raising issues an ethical company would want to know about, is simply not in the interest of the individuals or company involved. Waiting until the company's culture changes to support ethical inquiries is not a sound prospect. Consequently, leading corporations are setting up ethics inquiry services where inquiries are encouraged and kept confidential. When unethical acts are reported, they are quickly and fairly investigated, and the reporter's name is kept confidential unless and until the matter has to go to court. Even then, the reporting individual is asked if he or she will permit his or her name to be used. Quarterly or annual reports of inquiries and follow-up are made to very senior officers and to a subcommittee of the board of directors without revealing the names of the reporting individuals. These practices are essential to allay the often well-founded fears of the inquirers and reporters.

These ethics inquiry systems and protected whistle-blower programs are often under the jurisdiction of the organization's ethics officer, ombudsperson, human resources office, internal audit, or legal departments. Care should be taken not to send signals that would turn away employees from using the service. In this regard, locating the service within an internal audit department or legal department is not as attractive as locating it within a human resources department or as a stand-alone unit. A hotline to an undisclosed or third-party destination may also be suspect depending on the perception of its efficacy, trustworthiness and credibility. Over 50 percent of the inquiries received by existing services are seeking information on personnel policies and practices, so basing the inquiry system in an human resource related or stand-alone unit that specializes in these matters is recommended.[3] While this may give rise to a harmful conflict of interests in regard to poor human resource activities or policies, experience has shown this to be relatively rare compared to the volume of information-seeking calls.

Creating an On-going Monitoring or Review Mechanism

No significant ongoing process should be initiated without establishing a periodic process for monitoring performance, and ensuring consideration of changes that could bring continuous improvement. This should start with a review of the stated objectives for the ethical corporate culture, and the performance characteristics that were expected at the beginning of the review period. In the case of an ethical corporate culture this review should be undertaken at the direction and for the review of the ethics subcommittee of the board, by the chief ethics officer and the chief internal auditor, or those who occupy similar functions. Since the review mechanism is part of the maintenance process, it will be dealt with more fully in the next Chapter.

Employee and Management Compliance

Chapter 5 recommended having employees sign ethics compliance cards during the launch of the mission statement. This process is considered important because it focusses the attention of employees on the mission statement and code of ethics or conduct and requires them to confirm that they have read it, understood it, and that they will follow it. Periodic re-signing of compliance cards is also recommended because it will act as a reminder of the mission statement and related code and what it is trying to achieve. Consideration should be given to extending the sign off notification beyond an employee's own actions, so that when signing off, he or she would be confirming that they know of no other employee or corporate action that is unethical that has not been reported.

---

3. For further information see for example, Leonard J. Brooks, "Whistleblowers – learn to love them!" *Canadian Business Review* Summer (1993): 19–21.

Senior management and the board of directors, as mentioned in Chapter 3, lead and support the development and maintenance of an ethical corporate culture. Processes designed to evaluate management and board performance should take into account how effectively such leadership and support has been provided with regard to the items noted below:

- The ethics program generally
- Communications processes established
- Employee training programs, including lunch and learn sessions
- Reinforcement and compliance initiatives
- Processes designed to obtain employee feedback and to follow-up on such feedback
- Processes designed to address violations and actions taken
- Processes designed to address new concerns and issues
- Integration of ethical performance goals into job descriptions and remuneration systems

The effectiveness of the chief ethics officer and his or her supporting ethics committee should also be evaluated with regard to reporting and actions taken.

Addressing violations of the code of ethics

An appropriate process should be designed to address violations of the code of ethics. This process should consider:

- Who within the organization should address violations
- How employees involved with violations should be disciplined both with regard to the investigation and hearing processes, and the level of penalty to be assessed in the event that allegations are found to be true
- How the violations will be communicated to all employees and other stakeholders

The seriousness of the violation, how senior the alleged perpetrator is, and the effect on the organization and its reputation may determine the process that is followed and whether senior management or the board of directors actually become involved. However, since it is advisable for employees to believe the investigation and hearing processes are fair, timely, and credible, an organization should create and announce a standard process which is administered by the chief ethics officer.

Except where the violation has legal implications or a desire to protect the name of the violator, the nature of the violation and penalty should normally be made public, and compared to the company's guidance on the matter. As indicated in Chapter 2 in the discussion of the 20/60/20 Rule, since roughly 60 percent of employees will respond ethically if presented with proper guidance, knowledge of the nature of the violation and related penalty – from warning to termination – will reinforce ethical behaviour and add substantially to the culture of integrity the organization wants to maintain. Without such disclosure, rumours will abound about how the perpetrator got off, or how the company swept the matter under the rug, for a variety of reasons. Sometimes insurance companies that are attempting to induce or enhance recoveries will press for non-disclosure, but the advantages cited should be weighed against the cultural benefit provided by disclosure. Legal action may be required if a law is actually violated.

Reinforcement and Compliance Summary

To reinforce employee understanding of the mission statement or code of ethics, an ongoing management communications program is needed. Workshops to develop management capability are recommended. Refresher workshops should be part of the training program, at least annually, and ethical issues and treatments should be integrated into general training programs. Feedback opportunities should be provided, as well as a way of effectively responding to the feedback and resolving issues. Achieving compliance with the mission or code involves recognition of strong ethics performance and documenting of intent to comply with the code. It also is reinforced by management reviews of each manager's contribution to the ethics management program. Lastly, ethics inquiries and violations must be effectively gathered, managed, and discipline appropriately applied. Procedures for measuring, monitoring, and reporting performance will support these essential activities.

For further information on compliance programs, refer to the following websites:

- Ethics & Compliance Officer Association at: http://www.theecoa.org
- Nike: http://nikebiz.com/responsibility/cr_governance.html

	Checklist – *Maintaining an Ethical Corporate Culture*
	Reinforcement & Compliance
✓	Reinforcement
	Effective Reinforcement of Values
	• Identify responsibility
	• Commitment of leaders
	Management Communications Concerning Ethical Conduct
	• A visible contribution by the CEO at the beginning
	• Letters by the CEO to senior management, all employees, suppliers, contractors, customers and shareholders should include, introduce, and link communication to the organization's values
	• A periodic ethics reminder letter can be sent from the CEO to employees, customers, agents & suppliers on a quarterly or semi-annual basis
	• The chief ethics officer reports to the ethics, governance, or audit subcommittee of the board on the status of the company's ethics program, any instances or patterns of conduct worthy of revised guidance or action, any trends noted in environmental scans that will impact the company, and any suggested revisions to the ethics program
	• The annual report and annual meeting should include reports from the CEO & directors on how the ethics program is being managed
	• Speeches given by the CEO should include a reference to the code and ethical issues, whenever appropriate
	• Employee newsletters should include discussion of relevant ethical issues
	• Company forms and reports should be modified to reflect the mission statement or code of ethics
	• A company website could be established to house the code, updates, news events, and awards for good performance
	• Communications from senior management on specific issues, particularly on strategic and tactical plans, contain references stressing compliance with the organization's code of conduct
	Reinforcement through management capability development
	• Periodically review the code of ethics & criteria, tools, and processes that may be discussed for identifying and resolving ethical issues
	• Discuss relevant ethical issues with a view to determining whether they were handled properly, whether feedback mechanisms were effective, and whether the code needs to be revised
	• Hear from, and provide feedback to, the corporation's ethics officer on the matters noted above for reporting to the board subcommittees
	Reinforcement through an annual ethics training program
	• Enhanced and updated from past years, covering current problems
	Reinforcement through integration into general training
	• Directors' and senior officer sessions

Reinforcement through feedback facilitated by:
• Appointment of an ethics officer, or an ombudsperson
• An ethics inquiry hotline
• Ethics committees
• Subcommittee of the board of directors for general oversight
• Employee assistance programs
• A protected whistle-blowing program designed internally, or out-sourced, to induce the greatest level of employee trust
Effective feedback processes have:
• Sufficient resources to permit follow-up
• Documentation of feedback received
• Criteria to help establish priorities
• Policies concerning confidentiality
• Management involvement when policies are challenged on ethical grounds
• Feedback to the individual who raised the matter, and when relevant, to all employees
Reinforcement through recognition
Reinforcement through job descriptions and reward systems
Reinforcement through Whistle-blower Programs & Inquiry Services
• Whistle-blower anonymity
• Whistle-blower protection
• Rapid & fair investigation
• Confidentiality of findings
• Quarterly or annual reports of inquiries and follow-up made to very senior officers and to a subcommittee of the board of directors
An ongoing Monitoring or Review Mechanism
• Responsibility assigned
• Report to board subcommittee
Employee and Management Compliance
• Sign off of compliance cards when hired
• Annual sign off
Evaluation of effectiveness of the Chief Ethics Officer and his or her supporting ethics committee with regard to reporting and actions taken with regard to the items noted below:
• The ethics program generally
• Communications processes established
• Employee training programs, including lunch and learn sessions
• Reinforcement and compliance initiatives
• Processes designed to obtain employee feedback and to follow-up on such feedback
• Processes designed to address violations and actions taken

	• Processes designed to address new concerns and issues
	• Integration of ethical performance goals into job descriptions and remuneration systems.
Addressing violations of the code of ethics	
	• Identification of responsibility for addressing violations
	• Fairness & speed of hearing process
	• Adequacy of penalties assessed
	• Communication about violations to all employees and other stakeholders

Maintaining an Ethical Corporate Culture

Chapter 7
Monitoring & Reporting Ethical Performance

Monitoring ethical performance effectively requires an evidence-based process that evaluates whether the organization's ethical performance objectives are being met in practise. In addition, an organization should consider how its corporate social responsibility (CSR) should be reported, whether the report will be designed to external general standards or company defined standards, and whether it should be verified or audited, and in what manner.

From a stakeholder perspective, ethical behaviour has to do with how the rights and interests of stakeholders are respected, and CSR reporting provides evidence of how this respect is demonstrated.

Each corporation should decide which elements of CSR are to be reported internally, and which are to be reported to the public. The precise nature and degree of disclosure will determine the image of corporate citizenship that the corporation will take on.

Measurement of CSR

The measurements chosen for CSR should highlight key factors that will contribute to the strategic objectives of the corporation. This will involve defining what the strategic objectives are, and what they require in terms of the support needed from both domestic and foreign stakeholders. In addition, CSR measurements should be chosen to facilitate reports for customers, such as government purchasers, that may require CSR details such as the percent of women and minorities on staff or details of loans to minorities, for bids or assurance of CSR processes. Finally, several organizations are developing standardized CSR reports, and their efforts should be reviewed before finalizing a corporation's CSR measurement and reporting protocol.

Measurements or indicators of CSR can take many forms. There are a number of organizations[1] that rate the CSR of many companies, and their list of criteria can be used as a guide in establishing an appropriate list of measures. For example, indicators of historical fact, based on voluntary surveys sent to senior corporate officers, are used by the Corporate Ethics Monitor[2], including:

- Existence of statements of guidance, their currency, and reinforcement
- Employment record, including total staff, number of women and minority group members in board or management positions
- Amount of charitable donations in relation to other companies in the sector, and allowing comparison to profits as a means of assessing relative generosity
- Existence and nature of community relations programs
- Labour relations and health and safety
- Environmental management indicators
- Environmental performance indicators
- Ethical sourcing and trading policies

There are other measures that may be useful in revealing attitudes of managers and employees toward ethical issues. These may be useful in capturing information about actions that are about to happen, or about changes in attitude due to certain signals sent voluntarily or involuntarily by management, or read into circumstances by employees. Examples of such anticipatory measures are:

- Employee attitude surveys such as those undertaken by Walker Information[3]
- Customer or other stakeholder surveys
- Evaluation by paid shoppers or solicited customer comments

Other measures concentrate on the operational merit of the organization's

---

1. See for example: in the US – KLD Research & Analytics, Inc. at http://www.kld.com, in Canada – EthicScan Canada at http://www.ethicscan.ca and Jantzi Research at http://www.jantziresearch.com, and in the UK – Ethics Investment Research Service (EIRIS) at Email: ethics@eiris.win.uk.net.
2. The *Corporate Ethics Monitor* is published by EthicScan Canada: http://www.ethicscan.ca
3. Walker Information's website is http://www.walkerinfo.com

support mechanisms for ethical behaviour. This could include quality assessments of:

- Codes of conduct
- Training programs
- Reinforcement mechanisms, including:
  - Newsletters, correspondence
  - Pay and reward systems
  - Promotion
  - Protection for whistle-blowers
  - Follow-up on reported problems
  - Speed and fairness of investigation, hearing, and of penalty assigned

Measures are also available to indicate:

- The level of understanding that employees have of ethical issues[4]
- The principal motivator for an employee's ethical behaviour[5]
- Whether an employee is disposed to raise ethical concerns due to his or her perception of his or her ability to affect the outcome of such debates (locus of control tests[6])
- The degree of inclusion of ethical concerns in, "the development of plans, setting of goals, search of opportunities, allocation of resources, gathering and communication of information, measurement of performance, and promotion and advancement of personnel"[7]

Table 1: Techniques for the Measurement of Ethical Processes & Performance is offered at the end of this chapter to put into perspective how these

---

4. See for instance, the Defining Issues Test (DIT) as discussed in James R. Rest, *Development in Judging Moral Issues* (Minneapolis: University of Minnesota Press, 1979.)
5. According to the subject's stage of moral reasoning per the schema developed by L. Kohlberg in *Essays in Moral Development, Volumes I and II: The Psychology of Moral Development* (San Francisco: Harper & Row, 1981 and 1984.)
6. "Locus of control is a self-regulatory aspect of character that captures individuals' tendency to feel that control of their lives rests in their own hands (internal locus of control) or in the hands of others (external locus of control). Those who are "internals" take responsibility for their actions, and are therefore more likely to act upon their ethical judgment. "Externals" are less likely to take responsibility for their actions and, therefore, are more susceptible to the pressures of the situation, feeling somewhat powerless." from Joanne Jones, Dawn W. Massey and Linda Thorne, "Auditors' Ethical Reasoning: Insights From Past Research And Implications For The Future," *Journal of Accounting Literature* 2003.
7. Lynn Sharp Paine, "Managing for Organizational Integrity," *Harvard Business Review* March – April (1994): 112. (Reprinted as a reading at the end of the book.)

measures can be related to the attribute or process involved in maintaining an ethical corporate culture.

Monitoring CSR

The corporation that embarks on a CSR measurement program needs to consider how it will report on performance, whether the report will be internal only or available to the public, and who will be charged with the responsibility for reviewing the reports and pursuing program revisions on a continuous improvement basis. Internal reports can take on any form, but should be focussed on the program's performance objectives.

After the CSR measurements have been identified, the data gathered, and the report fashioned, the next step is monitoring how your corporation is doing. As with most measurement schemes, comparison can be helpful with:

- Strategic objective key success factors
- Similar organizations
- Best-practice alternatives for benchmarking
- Published standards such as those described above
- Industry statistics and averages
- Management by objective targets
- Results obtained in earlier periods

Ethical performance could also be selectively monitored by reference to external studies. These may be found in books like *The 50 Best Ethical Stocks for Canadians*[8], or in industry studies published in the *Corporate Ethics Monitor*. Alternatively, several annual studies are published such as the "100 Best Corporate Citizens" in *Business Ethics* magazine, or as it has now been absorbed into the *CRO, The Corporate Responsibility Officer* magazine. This publication also features its Annual Business Ethics Awards that identifies companies judged to be outstanding performers[9]. Even general business publications like the Economist offer useful, and sometimes skeptical information on CSR in surveys and editorials such as those in their January 22, 2005 issue. Organizations also exist, such as Toronto's Social Investment Organization (SIO), that provide information derived from CSR matters. On a specific company level, it is possible to obtain a specific report on the

---

8. Deb Abbey and Michael C. Jantzi, *2001 Edition* (Toronto: McMillan Canada, 2000.)
9. Another awards program providing similar sources of best practice is organized by *Corporate Knights Magazine*. The Best 50 Corporate Citizens in Canada Annual Survey can be found at http://www.corporateknights.ca/reports/

CSR performance of your company from research organizations like Jantzi Research or EthicScan Canada that are providing them to the corporate and investment community. Hiring a consultant specializing in ethical performance measurement may also be beneficial, especially if the consultant has extensive experience with ethical processes in other organizations that he or she can use, on a confidential basis, for benchmarking purposes.

Reports will be most useful when reviewed and analyzed on a continuing basis. The chief ethics officer and other individuals carrying out the review and analysis should be familiar with the ethical performance process, and should be committed to its improvement. They should be formally charged with, and known throughout the organization to have, the responsibility for improving the process and should also have the responsibility to report to senior levels of management and/or a subset of the board of directors. These individuals may be part of, or report to, an ethics advisory committee with ongoing responsibility and authority to revise the company's ethics program, and/or to a subcommittee of the board of directors. An interesting example of this is reported in the article,[10] reproduced as a reading for this chapter, by Prakash Sethi, who is the Chair of the Mattel Independent Monitoring Council for Global Manufacturing Principles.

Public Reporting of CSR

Recently, several organizations have created and published standards for CSR reports. They are currently testing and refining their creations and will be modifying them further. Consequently, it would be wise to maintain a watching brief on the following:

- Global Reporting Initiative (GRI) involves a comprehensive reporting framework (G3) covering economic, environmental and social performance that is being developed by a global group including noted stakeholder environmentalists, accountants and others – see http://www.globalreporting.org
- AccountAbility, a UK group, is developing the (AA1000) sustainability reporting framework that provides guidance on how to, "establish systematic accountability processes and how to assure how the underlying systems, processes and competencies live up to the AA1000 Assurance Standard" – see http://www.accountability. org.uk

---

10. S. P. Sethi, "Codes of Conduct for Global Business: Prospects and Challenges of Implementation," *Principles of Stakeholder Management* (Toronto: The Clarkson Centre for Business Ethics, 1999): 9–20.

- Social Accountability (SA) and Audit (SAA) has developed SA8000, a "comprehensive and flexible system for managing ethical workplace conditions throughout global supply chains," and SAI, a system for auditing SA8000 performance – see http://www.sa-intl.org

The G3 and AA1000 are particularly promising frameworks, and Tables 2 and 3 offer summaries on them at the end of this chapter.

Public reports are becoming more common. Reporting ethical performance can:

- Heighten awareness of ethical issues within an organization
- Provide encouragement for employees to adhere to ethical objectives
- Inform external stakeholders
- Enhance the image of the company

Internal reporting of ethical performance can take several forms. Newsletters can provide full or partial reports, scorecards as well as recognition of exemplary behaviour by employees. Other internal reporting systems could include charts or progress reports on bulletin boards, partial or full reports as stand-alone documents, and verbal or video reports by senior management. Written reports can be prepared by internal staff and certified by external agents like auditors, professors, or editors of ethics publications. Alternatively, reports can be prepared entirely by individuals independent of the corporation. Several organizations, including The Council on Economic Priorities Accreditation Agency (CEPAA) in New York and EthicScan Canada in Toronto, train auditors to review CSR/CEP activity; and large public accounting firms offer related services including Ethics and Integrity (KPMG), Reputational Assurance (Pricewaterhouse-Coopers), Governance Review (Ernst & Young) and Corporate responsibility and Sustainability (Deloitte & Touche). Details are available on each organization's website.

Large corporations are releasing ethical performance reports to the public with greater frequency on a continuing basis. Such reports may be a few paragraphs in the annual report and may, or may not, be specifically identified as ethical performance reports. For example, an annual report may separately comment on corporate governance issues, gender equality, employment of minorities, charitable donations programs, environmental issues, and health and safety issues. More companies are publishing separate reports specifically devoted to ethical conduct or specific components thereof. General Motors, Dow Chemical and BP were early examples of this. More recent examples are Shell, Placer Dome, and Royal Bank of Canada (among many others). Readers may access the web site for any significant public company and in many cases find public reporting of some kind on ethical issues. Such information can be particularly useful for companies wishing to start down this road, or to improve their reporting if they have already started. "Appendix A: CSR and Sustainability Reports, Indexes, and Rankings," and the accompanying website at http://www.ethicscentre.ca provide ready access to lists of companies:

- 25 companies with recent CSR reports per the GRI website
- 10 companies included in the Jantzi Social Index of October 2007
- 100 companies included in The 2007 AccountAbility Ranking
- 30 companies with CSR reports and related website addresses
- Over 300 companies included in the Dow Jones Sustainability Index World October 2007

The reports from Shell and VanCity Credit Union, which are both audited or externally reviewed, make very useful reading and can be accessed at http://sustainabilityreport.shell.com/servicepages/welcome.html and https://www.vancity.com/MyMoney/AboutUs/WhoWeAre/Corporate Reports/AccountabilityReport/ respectively. Environmental performance reports, it should be noted, are mandatory disclosure in some parts of Europe.

Senior management may not support reporting, especially to external parties, if the results to be reported are unfavourable or if the possibility of legal action is significant. This is, however, an evolving area. Stakeholders are becoming increasingly interested in ethical performance, and leading companies are responding. Organizations are recognizing that it can be to their benefit to report even when the results are unfavourable. On the other hand, even when unfavourable results are not reported, the motivation for improvement remains in that if corrective action is taken, favourable results can be reported in future.

Audit or Verification of CSR Reports

One of the recent developments noted above, although there have been isolated examples of earlier attempts to audit or verify CSR claims, is the spread of so-called audits of CSR reports, particularly in Europe. European initiatives in environmental protection and through the International Standards Association (ISO) have had a driving influence on corporate behaviour and have required public disclosure of environmental performance.

As a result, many individuals, and some large public accounting and other firms have become involved in attesting to the reports issued. Reports by BP, Shell, and VanCity Credit Union, for example, have been audited in whole or in part. Independent audits of labour practices in undeveloped and developing countries have become rather common for retailers and their manufacturers whose products come significantly from such sources, for example, Nike, Adidas and Umbro. Care should be taken when relying on certifications in this area because auditing standards have not yet become generally accepted for this kind of reporting. Increasingly, however, international accounting bodies and other organizations such as CEPAA and AccountAbility are focussing on the need for appropriate auditing standards, including standards for the content of audit reports and certifications. National and international professional accounting bodies are beginning to take a greater interest in these areas. As well, the next phase of ISO reporting may well push currently registered firms beyond documentation of systems to the reporting and audit levels. Articles are appearing that review different aspects of CSR disclosure.

It is possible for a corporation to have company personnel audit CSR reports. Internal audit staff may be used, as may managers from other divisions of a company. This managerial audit approach was used by Dow Corning and was lionized in Harvard Business School cases prior to the unfortunate breast implant scandal. It should be pointed out that the Chairman of the Conduct Committee of Dow Corning remains convinced of the worth of the company's ethics audit program, but acknowledges that audit improvements were warranted[11].

Questions provided in Table 4 below can be used to guide auditors of not just reports, but also auditors of an ethics program in which there is a written code.

Summary

The effective management of corporate ethical performance is facilitated by the measurement, monitoring, and reporting of performance. Attention to these aspects of an ethics program will go a long way toward developing and maintaining an ethical corporate culture, maintaining the support of stakeholders, and facilitating the achievement of corporate strategic objectives.

11. See, for example the quotation of the Chairman of the Conduct Committee of Dow Corning in the "Dow Corning Silicon Breast Impants Case" in L.J. Brooks, *Business & Professional Ethics for Directors, Executives & Accountants*, 4e, (Mason, Ohio: Thomson South-Western, 2007): 208, 209.

Readings *located at the end of the book*

S.P. Sethi, "Codes of Conduct for Global Business: Prospects and Challenges of Implementation," *Principles of Stakeholder Management* (Toronto: The Clarkson Centre for Business Ethics, 1999): 9–20.

Useful References

Richard M. Locke, Alvin J. Siteman Professor of Entrepreneurship and Political Science,

MIT *The Promise and Perils of Globalization: The Case of Nike* at: http://web.mit.edu/polisci/research/locke/nikepaperFINAL.pdf

Nike's website at: http://www.nikebiz.com/responsibility/cr_governance.html

Guideline for Corporate Social Responsibility (PLUS 9018), Canadian Standards Association (CSA), 2004.

Additional Readings and Useful References will noted on: http://www.ethicscentre.ca

TABLE 1: Techniques for the Measurement of Ethical Processes & Performance[13]

Attribute or Process / Measurement Techniques
Written objectives
Existence – broad, specific by function
Content – comprehensive set of values, clarity of coverage, relevance
Date of most recent revision
Annual sign off – yes/no, minimal or involving responsibility for reporting
Guidance given to directors, management, employees
Process – training sessions, workshops, and employees
Consultation with ombudsperson, others
Comprehensiveness of coverage (e.g., new employees)
Frequency, currency – board review, dissemination
Understanding of issues
Rating developed by persons responsible for ethics program for each level of employee
Some tests are available (e.g., defining issues test, stage of moral reasoning)
Inclusion of ethical concerns
Evaluation by management in decision making
In "the development of plans, setting of goals, search of opportunities, allocation of resources, gathering and communication of information, measurement of performance, and promotion and advancement of personnel"[12]

---

12. Lynn Sharp Paine, op. cit.

Frequency of coverage as agenda item
Commitment by all levels to the organization's ethical values
Rating by ombudsperson
Reports of ethical problems – fraud, customer and employee complaints
Visible encouragement by top management
Achievement of ethical objectives
Combination of – existence, stage of completion of plans, number of events, dollars spent, numbers experienced
Monitoring and continuous improvement
Identification of person(s) responsible
Adequacy of resources allocated
Periodic reports to senior management and Board
Evident action based on feedback
Effectiveness of reporting
Existence – internal, external
Impact analysis on employees and external stakeholders
Effectiveness analysis by researchers
Favourable/unfavourable mentions in the media

TABLE 2:   Global Reporting Initiative Sustainability Reporting Guidelines
            Standard Disclosure Framework – G_3 Version
            Overview of Topics Covered

Strategy and Analysis – CEO statement, key risks & opportunities

Organizational Profile – 8 items

Report Parameters – 17 items

Governance, Commitments, & Stakeholder Engagement – 17 items

Management Approach & Performance Indicators:

  Economic Performance (EC) – econ. perform., market presence, indirect impacts

  Environmental Performance (EN) – materials; energy; water; biodiversity; emissions, effluents & waste; products & services; compliance; transport

Social Performance:

  • Labor Practices & Decent Work (LA) – employment; labor/manage. relations; occupational health & safety; training & education; diversity & opportunity

  • Human Rights (HR) – manage. practices; non-discrimination; freedom of assoc.; child labor; forced & compulsory labor; security practices; indigenous rights

  • Society (SO) – community; corruption; public policy; anti-competitive behavior

  • Product Responsibility (PR) – customer health & safety; products & services; marketing communications; customer privacy

Source: Sustainability Reporting Guidelines [Draft], G3 version, Global Reporting Initiative, January 2006

TABLE 3: AA1000 Accountability Assurance Standard Summary

Purpose, Sustainability Reporting and Assurance:

- The AA1000 Assurance Standard is a generally applicable standard for assessing, attesting to, and strengthening the credibility and quality of a reporting organizations' sustainability reporting, and its underlying processes, systems and competencies. It provides guidance on key elements of the assurance process (is a standard guiding the audit of sustainability reporting).
- The AA1000 Assurance Standard is primarily intended for use by assurance providers in guiding the manner in which their assurance assignments are designed and implemented.
- Assurance should provide confidence in the report's underlying information to the reporting organization's stakeholders, particularly the direct users of the report.

Assurance of sustainability reporting prepared in accordance with generally accepted standards:

- The AA1000 Assurance Standard supports assurance (whether made public or not) of reporting that adheres to specific standards and guidelines, and is customised by the reporting organisation. It is specifically designed to be consistent with, and to enhance, the Global Reporting Initiative Sustainability Reporting Guidelines, as well as other related standards.

Commitment by reporting organizations:

- Reporting organizations commit to (1) identify and understand their environment, (2) respond to their stakeholders' aspirations, and (3) provide an account to their stakeholders regarding the organization's decisions, actions and impacts.

Assurance principles:

- Materiality: the assurance provider must evaluate if the report contain all the important information about the reporting organization's sustainability performance required by the organization's stakeholders for making informed judgements, decisions and actions.
- Completeness: the assurance provider must evaluate the extent to which the reporting organization can identify and understand material aspects of its sustainability performance.
- Responsiveness: the assurance provider must evaluate whether the reporting organization has responded to stakeholders' concerns, policies, and relevant standards; and adequately communicated these responses in the report.

Evidence (supporting the reported figures and disclosures):

- The assurance provider must evaluate whether the reporting organization has provided adequate evidence to support the information contained in the report.

Assurance statement (i.e. auditor's opinion):

- The assurance statement should address the credibility of the report and the underlying systems, processes, and competencies that deliver the relevant information, and underpin the reporting organization's performance.

- Elements of the assurance statement (i.e. auditor's report):
  - Statement on use of AA1000
  - Description of work performed
  - Conclusion on the quality of the report and underlying organizational processes, systems, and competencies
  - Additional comments if necessary

Assurance provider standards (i.e. auditor's independence and competencies):

- The credibility of a report's assurance relies on the assurance provider's competencies, independence, and impartiality.
  - The assurance provider should aim to be independent of the reporting organization and impartial with respect to the organisation's stakeholders. Any interests that detract from this independence and impartiality need to be transparently declared by the assurance provider.
  - The assurance provider must be impartial in its dealings with the reporting organization's stakeholders.
  - Assurance providers and the reporting organization must ensure that the individuals involved in any specific assurance process are demonstrably competent.
  - The organisations through which individuals provide assurance must be able to demonstrate adequate institutional competencies.

* For a full version of this report, visit: http://www.accountability21.net/

TABLE 4:   Ethics Audit Program Annual Audit Questions

Questions for each Business Unit

Responsibility:

- Is there a person at the business unit who is responsible for answering questions on, and administering the code? Who is this?
- Do the employees know of this person's responsibility with regard to the code?

Awareness and Commitment:

- Has the code been distributed to all employees and managers?
- Have all managers signed the representation letter confirming that, "during the past year, [they] and, to the best of their knowledge after due inquiry, [their] immediate subordinates who hold management responsibilities have complied with the code and also have taken appropriate actions to ensure compliance by other employees (who are [their] subordinates) and by contractors and consultants (whom [they] have engaged or are responsible for)?"
- Have all employees signed off during the past year, that they have observed the code and will continue to do so, and that they know of no unreported breaches of the code?
- Are all new employees signing off when they join the company?
- Do all suppliers, contractors, and consultants receive a written notification that it is understood they will abide by the code, or specific provisions of it, such as those on gifts or inducements, conflicts of interest, health and safety, or environmental protection?

Training:

- Do new employees receive training on the code when they join before they sign the code sign off?
- Have existing employees received training on the code during the past year? What is the nature of this training?
- Do suppliers, contractors and consultants receive a briefing on the code and their need to observe it?

Commitment and support provided by management:

- Has management above the business unit shown personal commitment and support for the code and the values on which it is based? How? (Speeches, memos, ...)
- Has the management of the business unit shown personal commitment and support for the code and the values on which it is based? How? (Speeches, memos, use in screening merit and promotion decisions, and so forth)
- Has there been reinforcing publicity in newsletters, or through publicity of good or bad examples of behaviour?

Operations:

- Do employees and managers have confidence in the business unit's systems for:
  - Answering ethics inquiries?
  - Bringing ethics concerns forward for investigation?
  - Investigation and sanction?

Survey 10 employees and 5 managers

- What are the annual usage statistics of each system?
- Were any significant ethical problems not handled appropriately?
- Were actions taken on a timely and appropriate basis?
- Do any items or issues require clarification to avoid further problems?
- Are there any suggestions for improvement of the Ccode or the processes involved?
- Do timely periodic reports to division management exist covering the activities of these systems?
- Are all items reported?

Results

- Are there examples of company business decisions made that appear to contravene the code, or any other aspect of management's stated values?
- If so, were such matters openly communicated and explained? If they were not, cynicism about the Code will likely increase.

Questions to be asked of each Organizational Unit Overseeing a Business Unit Operation, Assessment and Continuous Improvement:

Are there personnel assigned, specify whom, and systems in place to monitor and ensure:
  - Compliance with the code in each business unit and at the division level
  - Effectiveness of the procedures for complying with the code in such matters as training, sign off, inquiry, investigation, and sanction

     o Assessment of operations and risks
     o Reinforcement and support
- Are necessary actions taken in a timely and appropriate manner?
- Are timely reports prepared for and reviewed by division management?
- Are objectives related to the code built into the divisional and business unit yearly operating objectives statements?
- Are appropriate actions taken and reinforced by division management?
- Is there appropriate reporting to head office to allow remedial action and solutions to be shared across the company?
- Does head office react and respond to feed-forward or requests for clarification?
- Has management above the division level shown personal commitment and support for the code and the values on which it is based? How? (Speeches, memos, ... ?)
- Are there any issues needing further clarification or suggestion?
- Are there any issues that should be reported to the board for information or action?

	Checklist – Maintaining an Ethical Corporate Culture
	Monitoring & Reporting Ethical Performance
✓	Measurement of CSR
	• Historical measures
	o Existence of statements of guidance, their currency, and their reinforcement
	o Employment record, including total staff, number of women, and minority group members in board or management positions
	o Amount of charitable donations
	o Existence and nature of community relations programs
	o Labour relations and health and safety
	o Environmental management indicators
	o Environmental performance indicators
	o Ethical sourcing and trading policies
	• Anticipatory measures
	o Employee attitude surveys such as those undertaken by Walker Information
	o Customer or other stakeholder surveys
	o Evaluation by paid shoppers or solicited customer comments
	• Quality assessments of
	o Code of conduct
	o Training programs
	o Reinforcement mechanisms, including:
	• Newsletters, correspondence
	• Pay and reward systems
	• Promotion
	• Protection for whistle-blowers

	• Follow-up on reported problems
	• Speed
	• Fairness of investigation, hearing, and of penalty assigned
	• Depth of involvement
	o Employees level of understanding of ethical issues
	o The principal motivator for an employee's ethical behaviour
	o Whether an employee is disposed to raise ethical concerns due to his or her perception of his or her ability to affect the outcome of such debates (locus of control tests)
	o The degree of inclusion of ethical concerns in, "the development of plans"
	Monitoring CSR
	• Internal reports
	• External reports
	• Comparative assessment of results with:
	o Strategic objective key success factors
	o Similar organizations
	o Best-practice alternatives for benchmarking
	o Published standards such as those described above
	o Industry statistics and averages
	o Management by objective targets
	o Results obtained in earlier periods
	• Report to Board
	Public Reporting of CSR
	• Consider
	o GRI (G3)
	o AccountAbility (AA1000)
	o SA 8000
	• Audit or Verification of CSR Reports
	o External Audit Firm
	o External·individual or committee
	See also Tables at end of Chapter

Special Topics

Chapter 8
Making Ethical Decisions

Several factors have stimulated interest in making ethical decisions that assist rather than harm an organization. Just as corporations have seen the logic in reducing the risk of unacceptable behaviour through the introduction of ethical guidance as part of their governance program, they are extending their guidance regime to provide ethical decision aids and frameworks. Leaving employees to their own values and interpretations of codes of conduct leaves corporations exposed to risks of:

- Unethical behaviour
- Damage to reputation
- Diminishment of profit
- Failure to keep the support of key stakeholders
- Failure to achieve the organization's strategic objectives

The discussion of ethical decision making that follows builds upon the discussion in Chapter 2 of corporate accountability to stakeholders, not just shareholders, and of reputation and its role in maintaining the support of key stakeholders. Not only do employees have to understand why and how their company expects them to behave, they need to know what questions to ask to identify the important aspects of the impact of their decisions they need to take into account, and how to do so, before they make mistakes. The approach taken to a decision, and the decision framework applied, can be essential in later justifying a decision, and avoiding a disaster.

Ethical Decision Aids and Frameworks

In a sense, a code of conduct, and some codes of ethics provide an ethical decision aid or framework. However, codes do not cover all possible eventualities explicitly. If they did, their authors could superhumanly foresee future business developments, and the codes would be so lengthy that few would read and remember their contents. That is why it is far more practical to develop a code of conduct that puts forth values or principles that can be interpreted to assist in future decisions as they arise, rather than just an exhaustive set of rules to be matched against problems. However, the code cannot be so broad as to leave employees nonplussed as to how to act. When the code is unclear or ambiguous for an employee making a specific decision the employee needs to know where to turn for help, and needs to be aware that simply shrugging and taking the course of least resistance is not appropriate. These situations can be limited to a certain extent by providing examples in the code, supporting documents, and related training that clarify how to use the principles put forth, and each corporate department can identify examples that can make the principles more relevant. Keeping these updated is also very important.

In addition, as noted above, employees need guidance to ensure that they ask all the questions required about proposed actions sufficient to ensure that their decision can be made based on a comprehensive set of information. Failing to ask one important question can leave the resulting decision ethically vulnerable.

Several approaches or frameworks exist for a company to ensure that its employees will recognize ethical problems and analyse them fully, or at least know whom to consult. For example, it would be wise for a company to have its employees consider their decisions and activities using a two-stage process – a quick "sniff" test stage followed by a second stage more thorough consideration of impact on stakeholders using a rigorous framework such as stakeholder impact analysis, if needed. These two approaches are discussed below.

Sniff Tests and Common Rules of Thumb

It is often appropriate for managers and other employees to be asked to check a proposed decision in a quick, preliminary manner to see if an additional full-blown ethical analysis is required. These quick tests are often referred to as sniff tests. Commonly applied sniff tests include:

- Would I be comfortable if this action or decision were to appear on the front page of a national newspaper tomorrow morning?
- Will I be proud of this decision?
- Will my mother be proud of this decision?

- Is this action or decision in accord with the corporation's mission and code?
- Does this feel right to me?

If any of these quick tests are negative, employees are asked to seek out an ethics officer for consultation, or perform a full-blown analysis of the proposed action. This analysis should be retained, and perhaps reviewed by the ethics officer. A reading on "Sniff tests" is attached at the end of this book[1].

Many executives have developed their own rules of thumb for deciding whether an action is ethical or not. For example, Carroll[2] identifies the following six rules as important, according to practicing managers:

Golden Rule:
- Do unto others as you would have them do unto you.

Disclosure Rule:
- If you are comfortable with an action or decision after asking yourself whether you would mind if all your associates, friends, and family were aware of it, then you should act or decide.

The Intuition Ethic:
- Do what your "gut feeling" tells you to do.

The Categorical Imperative:
- You should not adopt principles of action unless they can, without inconsistency, be adopted by everyone else.

The Professional Ethic:
- Do only what can be explained before a committee of your professional peers.

The Utilitarian Principle:
- Do "the greatest good for the greatest number."

Unfortunately, although these rules of thumb are often very useful, they rarely, by themselves, represent a comprehensive examination of the decision and therefore leave the individuals and corporation involved vul-

1. Leonard J. Brooks, "Sniff Tests," *Corporate Ethics Monitor*, 7:5 (1995): 65.
2. A.B. Carroll, "Principles of Business Ethics: Their Role in Decision making and Initial Consensus," *Management Decision*, 28:8 (1990): 20–24, see Figure 3.

nerable to making an unethical decision. For this reason, the more comprehensive techniques of stakeholder impact analysis should be employed whenever a proposed decision is questionable or likely to have significant consequences. Normally, this more sophisticated analysis would be performed by, or with the assistance of, an ethics officer or by senior management.

Stakeholder Impact Analysis

Assessing the impact of a proposed action on the stakeholders to be affected by the decision, known as stakeholder impact analysis, can be undertaken in several ways, but these can be reduced to examining three fundamental aspects of the impact. Interestingly, in 2004 the AACSB, the worldwide accreditation body for schools of business, released an Ethics Education Task Force Report[3] that calls for business school students to be educated in making ethical decisions using the three approaches identified in Figure 8.1. It is essential to note that an ethical decision may not result unless all three approaches are applied effectively.

The first approach, or consequentialism stage, examines the consequences or usefulness of a proposed decision. Consequences must be considered for each stakeholder group – not just for shareholders. This is quite different than what many companies require. While a corporation's shareholders may be considered the most important stakeholders, the realization that achievement of strategic goals requires the support of key stakeholders necessitates the consideration of their interests and the impacts upon them. This consideration can take the form of computation of projected net profit or contribution for shareholders, and/or projected costs and benefits for other stakeholders. Such projections can even be adjusted for risk or probability of occurrence of related events. A decision would be considered potentially ethical if the net profits and net benefits (benefits-costs) are positive.

The next stage[4] of analysis involves the examination of the impact of the proposed decision on the duties, rights, or interests of all stakeholders. Relevant questions could be:

- Are all fiduciary duties owed by company personnel to other stakeholders properly discharged?

---

3. AACSB EETF Report, 2004, (Report of the Ethics Education Task Force: Ethics Education in Business Schools, Association to Advance Collegiate Schools of Business), see http://www.aacsb.edu
4. Referred to as deontology as it has to do with the study of obligations.

Figure 8.1
Ethical Decision-Making Approaches and Criteria

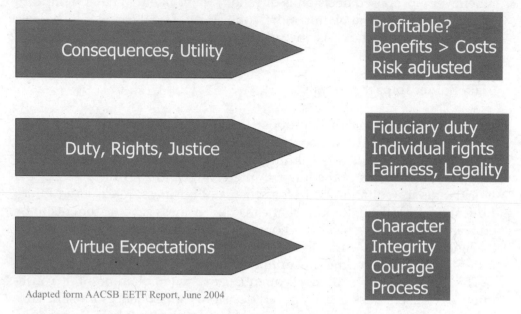

Adapted form AACSB EETF Report, June 2004

© 2007 L.J. Brooks.   Reproduced with permission from
Business & Professional Ethics for Directors, Executives & Accountants, Thomson South-Western

- Are property, legal, and other rights (for example, health, safety, life, fair treatment, freedom of speech) respected?

A decision would be considered potentially ethical if all stakeholder duties and rights were discharged and/or respected.

The final or virtue expectations stage of analysis considers whether the behaviour of company personnel and its agents that is inherent in the proposed decision matches stakeholder expectations. Has the company, or its personnel and its agents demonstrated the virtues expected of them? Have they demonstrated the honesty, integrity, forthrightness, courage, compassion, and other aspects of character that their stakeholders expected in their company's decisions, activities, or processes? For example, although a line of car tires has not been declared unsafe by regulators, has the manufacturer informed customers about abnormally high incidences of blow-outs or instituted a recall? Or, has a company mistreated animals in its testing processes? A decision to act (or a decision not to act) would be considered potentially ethical if the virtues expected were delivered.

Only after the three stages of analysis have been completed do we know if each stage has yielded a positive or ethical verdict. It may be that a proposed decision is profitable, but not fair to all stakeholders. Or a proposed action could be profitable, but not live up to the expectations of customers or employees – who are disenchanted and buy elsewhere or change employers, or work with lowered enthusiasm or effectiveness thus lowering profits in the longer term. Accordingly, a proposed action cannot be considered ethical unless and until all three analytical approaches are completed and the results found to be positive. Fortunately, if the results of one of the tests are negative, the proposed decision can be revised on an iterative basis until the negative aspect is removed[5], if possible.

It is unlikely that a stakeholder will be favourably disposed to a decision that leaves him or her worse off, so looking for an alternative that leaves everyone better off is best, and one that leaves no one worse off is also desirable. Unfortunately, it is not always possible to find such a solution, which means that some stakeholders may have to be worse off. In this case, the question to be asked is whether, taking all stakeholder impacts into account, the overall impact of the proposed decision will be a net benefit or a net cost.

If the overall net impact of the proposed decision is positive, there is still a question of whether the decision is fair to all stakeholder groups. If not, some stakeholders will be worse off, and the question is whether the overall gain warrants disadvantaging some. Again, the extent of this disadvantaging or unfairness will have to be assessed to see if the trade off is warranted.

One way to assess the degree of unfairness is to examine what impact the proposed decision will have on the rights of the decision maker, the corporation, and the other stakeholders. The rights attributable to stakeholders depend partly upon several factors including the culture of the individuals affected, and the law of the country involved. However, there are some rights that are generally held to be universal, particularly in North America, and worldwide by North American stakeholders. They include the right to the following:

- Life
- Health and safety
- Exercise of conscience
- Dignity and privacy

---

5. For an wider discussion of stakeholder impact analysis see Leonard J. Brooks, *Business & Professional Ethics for Directors, Executives & Accountants*, 4e (Thomson South Western, 2007), Chapter 5.

- Freedom of speech
- Freedom of association
- Fairness
- The keeping of agreements, including oral agreements

The Modified Tucker Framework

Sometimes the stakeholder impact analysis is distilled into decision frameworks or a set of questions that employees are encouraged to use when they are called upon to make decisions. One of the simplest of these is the framework that Graham Tucker suggested in the article in the readings section.[6] Tucker's framework, modified to incorporate a question on expected virtues, suggests that proposed actions be challenged by asking the following questions:

1. Is it profitable?
2. Is it legal?
3. Is it fair?
4. Is it right?
5. Does it demonstrate the expected virtues?
6. Optional question: Is it sustainable (environmentally/over time)?

A proposed action or decision that passes all challenges positively is ethical. Sometimes the challenges will reveal a negative which through redesign of the decision can be improved to be neutral or positive in impact. Often the proposed decision involves trade offs between two or more stakeholders, and therefore will rely upon the judgment of the decision maker and outside experts to arrive at the most ethical resolution.

There are some limitations to the Tucker framework that should be noted. It focusses on profit, which potentially is very short run in perspective. Moreover, profit doesn't take into account any externalities, such as pollution created that are not usually captured in traditional financial statements, at least in the short run, but are nevertheless the result of a corporation's actions and represent impacts on stakeholders. If the proposed decision under review involves a longer-term problem, or externalities, the assessment ought to be upgraded to include a cost-benefit analysis with an appropriately longer time horizon, or even more sophisticated techniques.

Another enhancement that should be considered is the assessment and

---

6. Graham Tucker, "Ethical analysis for environmental problem solving," *Agenda for Action Conference Proceedings,* the Canadian Centre for Ethics & Corporate Policy, 1990, 53–57.

Figure 8.2
Modified Tucker Framework for Stakeholder Impact Analysis

Questions To Challenge Actions or Decisions

1. Is it profitable?
2. Is it legal?
3. Is it fair?
4. Is it right?
5. Does it demonstrate the virtues expected?
6. Optional question: Is it sustainable (environmentally/over time)?

Modify using moral imagination and optimize

ranking of the severity of impact of the proposed decision on each stake-holder group. All impacts are not equal in severity of impact and therefore cannot be considered to be of equal consequence from an ethical perspective. For example, an employee's health and safety is not, in North America, considered to be of equal consequence to the earning of a profit for shareholders. Trading off an employee's health or safety for more profit would not be considered ethical. Similarly, disadvantaging vulnerable stakeholder groups such as children is frowned upon, as is advantaging a stakeholder group with lots of resources to disadvantage a group with very few resources. In assessing trade offs such as these, it is often wise to consider how the public, the media, and the corporation's primary stakeholder groups will view the impacts.

In addition to the article by Tucker, a more complete treatment of ethical decision making, including additional approaches and examples can be found in Chapter 5 of *Business & Professional Ethics for Directors, Executives & Accountants*[7].

Common Ethical Decision Making Pitfalls

There are several pitfalls that unaware decision makers fall into repeatedly. These include:

---

7. Op. Cit.

Focusing on short-term profit and shareholder only impacts

Often, the most significant impacts of a proposed action are those that surface in the future, and those that befall non-shareholder stakeholders. Frequently, only after non-shareholders react, do shareholders bear the cost for misdeeds. The remedy for this myopia is to ensure an adequate time horizon for the analysis, and to take into account all externalities on a cost-benefit basis even though the impact measured is felt initially by a non-shareholder group.

Focusing only on legalities

Many managers are only concerned with whether an action is legal. They argue, "If it's legal, it's ethical." Unfortunately, many find their corporation unnecessarily subject to consumer boycotts, employee slowdowns or inefficiency, increasing government regulation to cover loopholes, and fines. Some managers don't care because they are only intending to stay at the corporation for a short while. The fact is that laws and regulations often lag public expectations. One reason is that corporations lobby against such rule changes. For example, auto companies lobbied against the adoption of 21 miles per hour rear crash tests for over five years until the Ford Pinto lawsuits were settled. Caution is called for – just because a proposed action is legal does not make it ethical.

Limits to fairness

Sometimes decision makers only want to be fair to groups they like. Unfortunately for them, they do not have the ability to control public opinion and may end up paying for their oversight. Many executives have been put off by activist organizations such as Greenpeace, but have learned that environmental issues are ignored at their peril. A full review of fairness to all stakeholders is vital to ensuring an ethical decision.

Limits to rights canvassed

Bias influences decisions in many ways. Decision makers should canvass the impact on all rights for all stakeholder groups – not just their favourites.

Also, decision makers should be encouraged to take their own values into account when making a decision. Courts in North America no longer react favourably to the defense that, "I was ordered to do it by my boss."

Employees are expected to use their own judgment, and many jurisdictions[8] have set up protective whistle-blowing and "right to refuse" statutes to encourage employees to do so. Often, managers that force unfortunate actions on subordinates are really not acting in the best interests of shareholders anyway.

Conflicts of interest

Bias based on prejudice is not the only reason for faulty assessments of proposed actions. Judgment can be clouded by conflicting interests – the decision maker's personal interest versus the corporation's best interest, or the interests of groups the decision maker is partial to versus the corporation's best interest can both account for erroneous assessments and decisions.

Failure to identify all stakeholder groups, rank their interests, and understand their interconnectedness

The need to identify all stakeholder groups and interests before assessing the impacts on each is self-evident. However, this is a step that is repeatedly taken for granted, with the result that important issues go unnoticed. A useful approach to assist with this problem is to speculate on the downside of a proposed action, try to assess how the media will react, and how that reaction can lead to interest by other influential or legally powerful stakeholders. This often leads to the identification of and focus on the most vulnerable stakeholder groups who have the most urgent claims whose plight the media naturally tend to favour.

The media and public opinion will almost always side with employees rather than shareholders. For example, there was media and public outrage after the Enron bankruptcy when it was revealed that employees were exhorted to buy even more Enron stock when senior executives were selling theirs. Many lost their life savings. There was little evidence of similar outrage at the losses suffered by shareholders who were not employees.

Frequently decision makers fail to anticipate that what they do to one group will trigger action by another. For example, despoiling the environment in a far-off country can be picked up by domestic customers and capital markets on other continents due to TV shows with satellite feeds like CNN, or on Internet websites. Categorizing the interests or claims of stake-

---

8. See for example the New York State *Whistleblower Protection Law* that has been copied in many states, and the "right to refuse" statutes in Ontario labour, water, and pollution laws.

holders as urgent, powerful or influential, and legal or legitimate can be helpful in appreciating those interests likely to become most important to the achievement of the corporation's strategic objectives, and facilitate the decision-making process.

Competitors are Stakeholders Too

Much is written about the need for companies to act ethically towards their investors, employees, customers, suppliers, regulators and the environment. Less is written about the need to act ethically towards one's competitors. This may be because cutthroat no-holds-barred competition is still regarded as necessary by some business leaders for success in the capitalist system.

Many companies believe that competition must be fair, and some incorporate specific policies into their operating practices to prohibit unacceptable practices. Others do not. However, getting caught competing in a manner deemed unethical can result in bad publicity and law suits that can be very costly. It can also damage personal reputations. Two examples in the airline industry are illustrated in the case that follows.

Laissez-faire capitalism, based as it is on the presumption that competition is a good thing, inevitably generates the risk that it will be overdone. In most developed economies there are laws and regulations aimed at eliminating abuse, but there are many more areas that most stakeholders would regard as unethical, and could generate lawsuits.

Examples of unethical competition include:

- Direct theft of confidential data from competitors, such as customer lists and pricing information.
- Pressuring personnel formerly employed by competitors to reveal confidential information. Worse still, luring personnel from competitors for this purpose.
- Spreading unflattering or false information about competitors, either directly through advertising or indirectly by word of mouth to key stakeholders.
- Predatory pricing that creates losses until such time as a smaller competitor is driven out of business, at which time more monopolistic prices can be established.
- Conspiracies to deprive competitors of access to preferred suppliers.
- Disseminating information that products are of superior quality to those of competitors when it is known that they are not.

Illustrative Case: Two Airlines Caught Out

Two interesting and somewhat similar cases of unethical conduct have occurred in recent years in the airline industry.

In 1991, British Airways (BA) was caught stealing data from its major transatlantic competitor, Virgin Atlantic (Virgin)[9].They also sent employees to steal people out of Virgin's check-in lines by offering them cheaper (and unadvertised) fares. They were found out because a BA employee spilled the beans. The result was dreadful publicity and a major law suit that was settled for a substantial sum. The Chairman of BA, Lord King, subsequently resigned. Although ostensibly not for this reason, the press and the public were understandably skeptical. The important thing about this case is that nobody in the company, or in the media, ever attempted to justify this conduct as acceptable business conduct. The situation could presumably have been avoided if those in BA who instigated, or who knew about, these activities had called a halt either on ethical grounds or on the grounds that it was too risky and would be damaging if found out. Competition between BA and Virgin was exceptionally intense at that time. Virgin was an upstart enterprise run by an entrepreneur who had a very high (and favourable) public image. BA was a traditionally-run corporation with an excellent, but rather staid reputation, and it had previously had little or no real competition over the Atlantic from British companies. Their reaction may have been understandable, but not excusable, and internal structures should have been sufficient to prevent these events from occurring.

More than a decade later in 2004 it became known that a senior WestJet official had pressured a former Air Canada employee who still had password access to detailed Air Canada database information to provide that access to obtain flight scheduling information that would benefit WestJet's business. The individual was concerned about the propriety of this and asked for, and received, a signed indemnification from WestJet from any damages that might ensue. An employee eventually spilled the beans. A law suit ensued, which Air Canada settled, and Clive Beddoe, the Chairman of WestJet suffered damage to his personal reputation because it is alleged that he knew what was going on. Again, nobody has suggested that WestJet's conduct is appropriate business practice, but it is interesting that Beddoe stressed in defending his personal reputation that he had always run his business in an

9. "BA Dirty Tricks Cost £3m" BBC News online, http://news.bbc.co.uk/onthisday/hi/dates/stories/january/11/newsid_2520000/252018 9.stm

ethical manner[10] and he has apologized to Air Canada. This case raises the same issues as the earlier BA case, with the added element that corporate ethics has progressed significantly since then and that the primary focus of the response to being found out was to look to ethical metaphors to save his own, and his company's reputation. Of course, the other thing that the situation illustrates is that WestJet personnel were unfamiliar with the history of this kind of conduct in their industry. And as in the BA case, competition was intense, WestJet was viewed as an "upstart" and Air Canada's pricing policies had themselves been the subject of criticism in the past. In the end, though, this kind of conduct was universally deemed unacceptable and unethical.

Leaving out one of the Key Stakeholder Impact Analysis Approaches: Consequentialism, Rights and Duties, and Virtue Expectations

As pointed out above, a comprehensive ethical decision cannot be made if one of these three approaches is overlooked. Repeatedly however, decision makers short-circuit their assessments, and suffer the consequences.

Failure to exercise Moral Imagination

One of the most important steps in ethical decision making involves taking the time to assess whether there is a better or more ethical choice that can be made. This is called exercising moral imagination. Frequently, an outstanding improvement can be made. For example, Ford sold the Pinto in North America with a gas tank that ruptured on impact from the rear at 21 miles per hour or higher. In the UK, Ford sold a similar car named the Bobcat in which the gas tank placement was raised to avoid the rupturing problem, and thereby save many lives as well as the reputation and profits of Ford.

The disposal fiasco of the Shell Brent Spar oil storage vessel presents another example. The original decommission solution of sinking the huge storage tank in the deepest part of the North Sea was furiously opposed and stymied by Greenpeace, causing significant harm to the reputations and fortunes of Shell Oil. Ultimately, the 137 metre deep vessel was happily used to support a pier to dock ships in a fiord. Had this solution been iden-

---

10. On a 2004 conference call he is reported to have said, "I built this company based on integrity and honesty ..." Brent Jang and Paul Waldie, "What Clive Beddoe knew," Globe and Mail, October 3, 2006.

tified earlier through the exercise of moral imagination, all of the upset could have been avoided.

Steps for an Ethical Decision

In summary of the comments made on ethical decision making, the following steps should be taken when challenging a proposed action:

1. Identify all stakeholder groups and interests.
2. Rank the stakeholders and their interests, weighting the most important more heavily than other issues in the analysis. As discussed above, urgent claims like threats to life and health are generally considered more important than financial interests, and should be considered so by decision makers. Organizations should specify a ranking for key interests such as employee concerns, environmental concerns, and financial concerns.
3. Assess the impact of the proposed action on each stakeholder group's interests with regard to the consequences, rights and duties impact, and virtues expected:
   - Use a comprehensive framework of questions covering the following areas:
     - Consequences
       - Will the action generate a net profit or benefit?
     - Duty, rights, and justice
       - Is the action legal?
       - Is the action fair?
       - Does the action offend the rights of any stakeholders?
     - Virtue expectations
       - Does the action demonstrate the aspects of character that are expected, including integrity and courage?
   - Avoid the problems set out above, including:
     - Focussing on only short-term profit and shareholder impacts
     - Focussing only on legalities
     - Being fair only to groups management approve of
     - Ignoring the impact on the rights of the decision maker
     - Failing to identify and rank all stakeholder groups' interests
     - Leaving out one of the main elements such as virtues expected
     - Failing to exercise moral imagination
4. Iterate. Take the time to exercise moral imagination to optimize the decision.

Ethical Decision Making Aids

Some corporate executives have decided to provide their employees with ethical decision-making aids in an easily-carried form such as a pocket card. IBM and Bell Canada, for example, started with such a card. IBM now provides a website on the IBM Intranet to guide its employees. Both are good ideas.

An Illustration of Ethical Decision Making

Illustrative Ethical Decision Making Case – Dealing with Disappointed Apple iPhone Customers

On September 5, 2007, Steve Jobs, the CEO of Apple Inc, announced that the spectacularly successful iPhone would be reduced in price by $200 from $599, its introductory price of roughly two months earlier[11]. Needless to say, he received hundreds of emails from irate customers. Two days later he offered early customers who paid full price a $100 credit good at Apple's retail and online stores. Was this decision to mitigate the $200 price decrease, and the manner of doing so, appropriate from an ethical perspective?

If Apple management had used a *sniff test* prior to the decision, they might have come to the conclusion that their mothers wouldn't have been proud of or comfortable with it. Similarly, they might have discovered that the price reduction may have offended the Apple Code of Conduct for treatment of customers.

If Apple had considered the *stakeholder impacts* that the decision involved, they would have realized that, while past consumers would be most affected, the reputation of Apple would also be tarnished, and that could affect future consumers who they were trying to encourage. In addition, Apple employees – many of whom had been attracted by the strong Apple reputation for providing innovative solution of high quality – would question the company's motives, which could weaken their loyalty and commitment.

If Apple had applied *traditional ethical tests*, he would have found the following:

- Consequentialism
  From a profit perspective, Apple was expecting to more than offset the $200 per unit drop in margin with a gain in volume of sales. For the iPhone

---

11. David Ho, "Apple CEO apologizes to customers," *The Toronto Star*, September 7, 2007, B4.

alone, this may have been correct, but Apple has many products that are to be bought by other customers who could be affected negatively and who would see decision as an opportunistic price decrease from an extraordinarily high starting price. Gouging behaviour could be suspected, which would undermine Apple's wholesome value proposition and non-iPhone sales would suffer as a result. Overall, management might not be certain of making a combined net profit on sales of iPhones and other products.

- Duty, Rights and Justice issues
  Apple executives have a duty to make profits, as long as doing so doesn't violate any laws. In this case, early customers of the iPhone might have a legally enforceable right to sue for unfair practices, but individual actions would be far less likely than a class action. While the outcome is a matter of speculation, the prospect of further bad press that tarnishes Apple's image is of considerable concern due to the ripple affects noted above. The impact of unfairness of the price reduction could be magnified significantly by bad press. It is unlikely, although the early purchasers had the notoriety of having the newest technology available, that Apple management would have thought the $200 price reduction was fair if they had been personally affected.

- Virtues Expected
  In the minds of Apple's customers and employees, Jobs has an image of a far-sighted technical genius who has been driven to provide great value for his stakeholders, and this image has been transferred to Apple itself. For many stakeholders, the $200 price decrease doesn't match up to the expectations they have come to expect of Jobs or of Apple.

Apple might also have used the questions developed in the modified *Tucker Framework* to test the proposed $200 price decrease. If so, the answers could have been as follows:

1. Is it profitable? – outcome is not clear as discussed above
2. Is it legal? – probably, unless a consumer protection act is offended
3. Is it fair? – not accordingly to some customers and employees
4. Is it right? – no, according to some executives, employees, and potential customers
5. Does it demonstrate the expected virtues? – no, as discussed above
6. Optional question: Is it sustainable (environmentally or over time)? The environmental impact issue is not involved in this decision, but the medium and longer-term impacts are likely to be negative and may be significant. It would be unwise to repeat such a decision, or to ignore the possible future negative impacts to reputation.

On balance, Apple should consider the $200 price decrease to be unfair and unwise without some mitigation for early purchasers of the iPhone. Is the credit of $100 adequate, and its restricted use appropriate? Another analysis could be run, and a sound solution arrived at in an iterative fashion, applying moral imagination where possible. In this case it is probable that judgement will have to be applied. Time will tell. In any event, Jobs could have avoided the initial negative press and damage to his and Apple's reputation, if Apple had used the ethical decision making tools to analyse the decision before putting it into action.

It should be noted that, while price discounts of the type described in this case are not uncommon, and are not generally regarded as serious ethical problems, they have an ethical aspect that can be assessed using the ethical decision making approaches discussed in this chapter. They certainly represent risks which could weaken the reputation of executives and the company involved.

Readings *located at the end of the book*

Leonard J. Brooks, "Sniff Tests," *Corporate Ethics Monitor* 7:5, (1995): 65.

Graham Tucker, "Ethical analysis for environmental problem solving," *Agenda for Action Conference Proceedings*, the Canadian Centre for Ethics & Corporate Policy, 1990, 53–57.

	Checklist – Special Topics	
	Making Ethical Decisions	
✓	Ethical Decision Aids & Frameworks	
	• In use	
	○ Voluntary	
	○ Mandatory	
	• Training Session	
	• Refresher session	
	• Sniff tests	
	• Stakeholder Impact Analysis used to assess:	
	○ Identify all stakeholders' interests	
	○ Rank all stakeholders' interests	
	○ Potential consequences of decisions or actions	

	o Duty, right, and justice impacts
	o Demonstration of expected virtues
	o Overall Net Benefit
	o Sustainability
	o Moral Imagination
	o Iteration
	• Avoid Commons Pitfalls
	o Focusing on short-term profit and shareholder-only impacts
	o Focusing only on legalities
	o Fairness, but not for all stakeholders
	o Respect for rights, but not for all stakeholders
	o Conflicts of interest
	o Failure to identify all stakeholder groups, rank their interests, and understand their interconnectedness
	o Leaving out one of the Key Stakeholder Impact Analysis Approaches: Consequentialism, Rights and Duties, or Virtue Expectations
	o Failure to exercise Moral Imagination
	• Decision Aids
	o Do they exist
	o Are they online
	o Are they mandatory
	• Documentation & Reporting Guidance
	• Required Consultation if initial assessment indicates problems
	• Identification of knowledgeable counsellor (chief ethics officer)

Special Topics

Chapter 9
Conflicts of Interest

From a practical perspective, some of the most troublesome ethical problems faced by business people are those involving conflicts of interest. These are almost impossible to avoid, so the emphasis should be on increasing awareness of the dilemmas involved, and on how to minimize their impact.

A conflict of interest is a situation in which an individual is motivated to action or inaction by an interest other than the interest that is appropriate in the circumstances. For example, purchasing agents should make decisions for the benefit of their employer, and they should not allow a supplier to charge more than a fairly- bargained price for goods or services. Sometimes suppliers try to obtain a higher price by offering purchasing agents an incentive to appeal to their self-interest. If this is accepted and acted on, the purchasing agent is placing his or her interest and the supplier's interest ahead of the employer's interest. This is contrary to the expectation of the employer of a fair day's work, and loyalty, for a fair day's pay.

Conflicts of interest may be real, potential or, perceived. A *real conflict of interest* exists when an improperly-motivated action is taken. A *potential conflict of interest* situation exists when there is an opportunity for one party to be induced to act for other than the right interests. An *apparent or imaginary conflict of interest*, on the other hand, occurs when a reasonable person might believe that a conflict of interest exists, even if it does not. For example, because the perceiver is unaware of, or does not believe in, any safeguards that might exist. Unfortunately, the fall out from a perceived conflict of interest can be as significant as from a real conflict of interest, and a vigorous, costly defence may have to be mounted to clear the air. Consequently, almost as much care must be taken to avoid perceived conflict situations as real or potential ones.

Figure 9.1
Types of Conflict of Interest

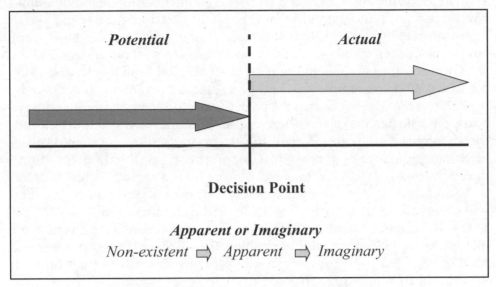

© 2007 L.J. Brooks.   Reproduced with permission from
Business & Professional Ethics for Directors, Executives & Accountants, Thomson South-Western

Main aspects of conflicts of interest

Usually conflicts of interest arise when the self-interest of a decision maker is placed ahead of the interests he or she should be representing. Most frequently, the main inducement for improper behaviour in conflict of interest situations is financial, but sometimes inducement comes from other beneficial arrangements for directors and employees, or their immediate families, from other organizations with which their employer does business. An example of a financial conflict is a purchasing agent whose spouse is a major shareholder in a supplier. An example of a non-financial conflict is when a senior officer is part of a decision-making process on an issue involving an organization that employs a family member. In not-for-profit and charitable organizations, conflicts are potentially very sensitive issues because of fiduciary responsibilities of directors, officers, and employees to those who provide the funding.

Conflicts of interest can also arise in relation to gifts and favours received and given. Also a conflict can arise when a person who has the responsibility for hiring finds applicants who are family members or friends. Conflicts will frequently arise when considering promotions or selection of personnel for termination or downsizing.

Misunderstandings can also give rise to conflicts of interest. Sometimes employees don't understand what they should be doing. They may be so intent on making a profit that they take unfair advantage of customers, employees, or other stakeholders, or break rules they don't understand the significance of, or both as in the case of RT Capital Management, Inc. On other occasions, an employee may be misled by errant managers, or by how things have been done in the past. Clearly, directors and officers have a responsibility to make sure there is clear guidance about important conflict of interests, and a supportive ethical corporate culture of shared values to ensure guidance is followed, or appropriate consultation on ethical questions takes place. Directors and officers have a responsibility to determine and articulate the conflict of interest strategy that their organization will observe, and then they must ensure that it is adhered to.

The RT Capital Management fiasco is a case where employees were manipulating 1998 stock market closing prices. Clearly the employees and traders involved were focussed on their own gains rather than on their fiduciary duty to the company's clients.

Fraud by Employees

Employee fraud[1] against an employer is relatively common, and is an example of a real conflict of interest in operation. Employees may also commit fraudulent, or otherwise illegal acts on behalf of their employer – *institutional or organizational fraud* – either because they believe they are acting in accordance with their employer's wishes (for example, paying a bribe to win a contract), or because they are instructed to do so. In both cases, an effective code of ethics that covers the issue should minimize the risk of occurrence, and in the latter case, a whistle-blowing mechanism may be effective if used by the employee. When an employee commits a fraudulent act ostensibly on behalf of the company, but in reality to obtain recognition and possible reward or promotion, for example by increasing his or her sales volume, then this fraud becomes a more straightforward conflict of interest situation. Enron and other recent corporate scandals are examples of both employee fraud against the company (i.e. excessive stock option gains) and institutional fraud on behalf of the company against

---

1. For purposes of this chapter, employee fraud consists of fraudulent acts by employees, and directors, against their employer.

others (i.e. misleading investors). Not surprisingly, literature on the subject of fraud is extensive.[2]

While many managers may believe that their associates and employees would rarely engage in unethical behaviour, forensic experts indicate that their experience suggests[3] that the general population can be divided into three groups:

- 10–20 percent would never bend the rules, steal or commit a fraud
- 80–60 percent would bend the rules if they thought they could get away with it
- 10–20 percent will seek to bend the rules, steal or commit fraud regardless of what controls are in place

The accuracy of these numbers is not as important as it is for management to realise that employee fraud is not rare, and that measures need to be taken to minimize the likelihood of its occurrence. That awareness, in itself, is an ethical action. It is unfair, for example, for a company to put unnecessary temptation in an employee's way by having poor internal controls.

Identifying potentially harmful situations and likely perpetrators

Recognizing High Risk Situations: The Fraud Triangle

Many forensic experts believe that the following three conditions need to exist before an employee will commit a fraudulent act against an employer. They refer to these as the elements of the *Fraud Triangle*[4].

1. There must be a *need*. For example, an employee who has serious financial problems will be more likely to steal resources from his or her employer than one who does not.
2. There must be an *opportunity* to commit the fraud with a low risk of getting caught. For example, a high risk of fraud occurring exists when an

---

2. See for example publications like the periodical *Report on Fraud* by Kroll Linquist Avey, now Navigant Consulting, published jointly by Navigant Consulting, Canadian Institute of Chartered Accountants, and the American Institute of Certified Public Accountants.
3. Based on discussions and presentations by experienced experts to the Diploma in Investigative & Forensic Accounting Program at the University of Toronto.
4. Fraud Triangle – see CICA Handbook Section 5135 or the new CAS 240; see also W. S. Albrecht, C.C. Albrecht and C.O. Albrecht, *Fraud Examination*, 2e, (Mason, Ohio: Thomson South-Western, 2006), 31.

employee has access to a valuable and marketable inventory over which there are poor controls.

3. There must be some way for dishonest employees to *rationalize*[5] their fraudulent behaviour. For example, the rationale for an employee stealing stationery or computer time might be, "everyone does it," or for padding an expense report, "my boss does it." A more general rationalization might be that the employee believes – sometimes with good reason – that his or her employer does not give a damn about its employees, or regularly cheats its customers or suppliers.

Removing Risk

The first condition, need, is largely beyond an employer's control, although the presence of counsellors to provide confidential advice and assistance to employees in financial and other difficulties may reduce the risk somewhat.

The second risk, opportunity, can be significantly reduced by a strong system of internal controls, particularly over cash and other valuable assets[6].

The third element, erroneous rationalization, can be mitigated by having a comprehensive and effective code of conduct and supporting policies. The code or policies must cover the matter in question comprehensively, for example, regarding use of company computers for personal purposes, or policy concerning use of airline reward miles earned on company business; and be effective in that employees must be aware of the rules, and that they are in fact applied consistently. Also, in general, it appears likely that employees will be significantly less motivated to commit fraudulent or other dishonest acts against the company if they believe its business is conducted on a high ethical plane.

---

5. For example, Joseph Heath, in his speech entitled "7 Neutralization/Rationalization Techniques" at the Centre for Ethics at the University of Toronto, April 9, 2007 mentions the following rationalizations:
   1. Denial of responsibility.
   2. Denial of injury.
   3. Denial of the victim.
   4. Condemnation of the condemners.
   5. Appeal to higher loyalties.
   6. Everyone else is doing it.
   7. Entitlement.
6. See for example, *Enterprise Risk Management – Integrated Framework: Executive Summary*, Committee of Sponsoring Organizations (COSO) of the Treadway Commission, September 2004, http://www.coso.org/publications.htm

Information Risks: Insider Trading Rules, Chinese Walls

Sometimes corporations are concerned that their employees will use or be seen to use information that is confidential, or that is to be kept confidential until a specific time. This is the situation that corporate insiders face when they know something before the stock market knows it, and therefore must not use it to their own advantage. Insider trading rules are set up to prevent employees from taking unfair advantage of this knowledge by delaying their use of information until appropriate disclosure has been made to the market. Corporations often lay down rules that extend the period during which insiders cannot trade to prevent the perception that insiders are misusing inside information.

"Chinese wall" is a term euphemistically used to describe barriers preventing information from passing from one part of an organization to another so as to prevent the misuse of that information. For example, a brokerage often will be involved in underwriting a new issue of securities, and the details of the pricing and timing are known in the underwriting department. This information would be of great value to the employees of the brokerage that serve the retail clients, because the clients could then buy or sell with perfect knowledge of the coming price of the securities. Obviously, this would be unfair to the other market participants, and therefore has been declared illegal. Great care is therefore taken to erect Chinese Walls to prevent such misuse of information – rules are put in place about who can not be told, who has access to files, how personal trades are scrutinized, how sign off declarations are used, and so on.

Agency theory and ethics

According to agency theorists, shareholders expect and hope that managers, and in turn, non-managerial employees will behave in line with the goals set for the corporation. In their terms, the principals or shareholders hope that their agents will be motivated to act as the principals wish. Incentive systems and punishment systems are created to try to influence the agents to stay on the right path and avoid situations involving *moral hazard*. Clearly, as the public's expectations for corporate performance now include ethical standards, the reward and punishment systems set up should also reflect ethical dimensions or shareholders are going to be disappointed. In fact, the corporation's strategic plans should include ethical dimensions to ensure that their agents, both inside and outside the corporation, are properly influenced, and conflicts of interest are avoided.

Management to avoid and minimize consequences

As indicated at the start of this section, conflicts of interest are almost impossible to avoid, so the emphasis should be on increasing awareness of the dilemmas involved, and on how to manage to minimize their impact.

Awareness Training

The first step in the process of managing to defend against these influences is to ensure that all employees are aware of their existence and consequences. This can be done through mission statements, codes of conduct, and related training. One of the items that should be covered in the training is the *slippery slope problem* where an individual can be enticed into a relationship by a seemingly innocuous request for a small favour, and then a larger one, and then find that they are told that unless they go along with a serious infraction, their past favours will be revealed. The start of the slope is too gentle for some to notice, but the slope becomes steeper and more slippery very quickly. In this area, it is important to set specific policies and communicate them. For example, personal use of air mile rewards earned on company business may be allowed or disallowed. If allowed, policies must include requirements to prevent employees taking unnecessarily circuitous routes to their destinations. The important thing is for employees, and their bosses, to know where they stand. The same applies to personal use of company computers. It may be totally forbidden, or it may be permitted, or even encouraged at designated times, and within certain limits of time and subject matter. Ford Motor Company attempted to resolve this matter imaginatively by giving their employees a personal computer of their own.

Understanding the Reasons Motivating the Training

The second step is to create an understanding of the reasons why the employer has developed guidelines to prevent conflicts of interest from occurring, their exploration though counselling if recognized, their reporting if they are identified as having occurred, and the penalties for their occurrence and non-reporting. These understandings can be reinforced by annual written confirmations of ethical behaviour and adherence to the employer's code of conduct that could include reference to conflicts of interest encountered by the signatory, and those identified involving others.

Guidelines and Consultation

The company's code of conduct should provide the rationale for avoiding conflicts of interest, what they are, how to avoid them, and what to do if an employee discovers that he or she is involved in one, or suspects that they might be. Consultation with a superior or an ethics officer is often warranted, and frequently used for clarification of issues of concern. Prior consultation is to be encouraged in order to avoid problems arising or becoming more serious.

Additional guidelines can be quite useful as supplements to codes of conduct. One helpful set of guidelines are those that clarify when it may be acceptable to give or accept a gift or preferential treatment. A useful series of questions to ask in this regard would be:

1. Is it nominal or substantial?
2. What is the intended purpose?
3. What are the circumstances?
4. What is the sensitivity (i.e. real or apparent culpability) of the recipient?
5. What is the accepted practice for the company or the country?
6. What is the firm or company policy?
7. Is it legal?

As indicated in the section on ethical decision making, these questions can act as sniff tests. If a problem is identified, then the employee, senior officer, or ethics officer should conduct a full stakeholder impact analysis using one or more of the decision-making approaches outlined above based on consequentialism and involving duty, rights, and fairness, as well as expected virtues.

Reinforcement, Monitoring and Compliance

Conflicts of interest can undermine an organization's values and reputation quickly and significantly. They must be featured in the company's reinforcement, monitoring, and compliance mechanisms on a regular basis so that company employees, officers, and directors remain sensitized to potential conflicts of interest, and aware of the remedies and the penalties for involvement. Company personnel must appreciate that conflicts of interest are an important dimension of the annual sign off and company monitoring mechanisms.

Useful References

Canadian Institute of Chartered Accountants, *Conflict of Interest: A Task Force Report*, (Toronto: September 15, 2000).

Navigant Consulting, *Investigations Quarterly(IQ)*, 2007– , *previously Report on Fraud, published by Navigant Consulting, Kroll Linquist Avey, the CICA and the AICPA*. 1999–2006.

Additional Readings and Useful References will noted on: http://www.ethicscentre.ca

	Checklist – Special Topics	
	Conflicts of Interest	
✓	Training Program/Ethics Workshop	
	• Includes conflicts of interest material identifying:	
	o Potential Conflicts	
	o Actual Conflicts	
	o Apparent or imaginary Conflicts	
	• Includes conflicts of interest material on the management of:	
	o Potential Conflicts	
	o Actual Conflicts	
	o Apparent or imaginary Conflicts	
	• Includes material on:	
	o Employee fraud	
	o Institutional or organizational fraud	
	o The Fraud Triangle	
	o Information risks	
	▪ Insider training	
	▪ Chinese Walls	
	o Agency theory	
	Organizational Codes, Guidelines & Policies	
	• Include:	
	o Rationale for avoidance	
	o Management of risk	
	o Consultation with superior or ethics officer	
	o Guidance for gifts, bribes	

	• Reinforcement mechanisms
	• Monitoring mechanisms
	• Compliance mechanisms

Special Topics

Chapter 10
International Operations

When a corporation operates outside its domestic market, the guidance offered employees must be reconsidered as to:

- How their usual operating practices will impact on the local economy and culture
- Whether different local foreign practices such as widespread gift giving, or even bribery, should be permitted or banned
- The reaction to these operations by domestic stakeholders, and particularly by primary stakeholders,[1] including major customers and capital markets

Impacts on local economies and their cultures

Multinational corporations may have a significant impact on local cultures that they would not have domestically. For example, they may have significant impacts on local:

- Labour markets: wage rates, supply
- Raw material and other input markets
- Political and legal processes
- Environmental conditions
- Religious and social customs

---

1. According to current thinking about the role of stakeholders (see Chapter 2), the support of the corporation's primary stakeholders is necessary for the corporation to achieve its medium and long-term strategic objectives.

If a multinational ignores local religious or social customs, it and its workers may be accused of *cultural imperialism*, and may find it difficult to obtain cooperation for future activities. Similarly, by virtue of its size, a multinational may so dominate the locale that there may be an unintended domination of local governments, courts, or elections that again may produce a backlash at some point.

Conflicts between domestic and foreign cultures

Perhaps the most difficult problems arise when the values of the primary corporate stakeholders differ from those in the local foreign country. Differences noted in the media in recent years have included:

- Bribery. Although bribes are illegal virtually everywhere, they are accepted in practice in many countries, but only as long as they receive no publicity. Facilitating payments (see below) are accepted even more widely, and some regard them as akin to tips that are paid to service providers in most Western cultures.
- Use of child labour. This is viewed as an essential component of the economy in many poorer countries, yet it is considered as unacceptable by many in developed nations.
- Use of prison labour. This has been an issue in China, although some states in the U.S. and at least one Canadian province use prison labour.
- Unhealthy labour conditions. Fatal fires in Thai toy factories resulted in widespread publicity.
- Treatment of women. Attitudes towards women in the workforce differ significantly in different cultures.
- Support of repressive regimes through location of operations. There are arguments within the developed world as to whether there is a net benefit to those who live under oppressive regimes as trade and investment increase. The United Nations and individual governments establish boycotts of certain countries for human rights abuses, and consumers now boycott companies that do not avoid such abuses. Companies need to be careful to look beyond the local labour laws in a foreign country, and respect international and home government directives. It is also wise to consider adopting a policy to strive at all times to improve the lot of those they employ or deal with, or at least to not take a direct part in the repressive aspects of a regime's practices.

- Respect for environment. The issue in this case is usually that environmental standards are lower in many undeveloped countries, or the standards are not effectively enforced.
- Dealings with family members. What in the West we might call nepotism may be regarded in some countries as acceptable, or even desirable.

Operating in foreign jurisdictions can lead to unexpected ethical dilemmas, and the need to modify application of an organization's code to take account of these circumstances. An illustration of this follows.

Illustrative Case: Making the Best of Bad Choices

This case illustrates that it is sometimes necessary to temporarily abandon established ethical principles to bring about a greater good. But this needs to be done rarely, and must be well-thought out and justifiable.

Some years ago a multinational company wished to operate a mine in a Third World country. To get permission, they had to come to terms with the needs of the native tribe that lived in the area. The company was convinced that the benefits in infrastructure and income to the local population were positive, and the locals agreed and were enthusiastic. After much negotiation they reached an agreement. In due course, the signing ceremony was arranged, dignitaries from the company, from the host government, and the local tribe were present. Then, at the very last minute, the chief approached the head negotiator for the company with an extra demand – the company should agree that it would not employ on the project anyone from the next tribe down the river!

How to deal with this? The company had a firm principle that it would not discriminate in employment on grounds of, among other things, ethnic origin. Agreeing to this would clearly breach this principle. On the other hand, holding up the signing ceremony, and potentially the project, on this issue would do enormous harm to a range of stakeholders. So a decision was made, and subsequently carefully documented, to agree to this change on the grounds of supporting the greater good. At the same time an internal commitment was made to try to persuade the tribe to change their attitude during the course of the contract, or as soon as possible. There was of course a risk that this would not succeed, but on the other hand there was the possibility that, if they were successful in changing their minds the company might have achieved an improvement in relations between two tribes with currently hostile relations.

This case illustrates that companies may consider acting contrary to specific principles when to do so would result in a greater good to most stakeholders and do no serious harm to others. When this is necessary, however, it is essential that the decision be made with the *utmost care and consideration*. In the above example, the decision was relatively easy because the alternative would have potentially been catastrophic for all concerned. The company may also choose to benefit the disadvantaged tribe in some other way. In other cases, the decision will be more nuanced, but the principles remain the same.

Corporations may locate operations in a country primarily because they want access to cheap labour, or lower environmental protection costs, or less governmental red tape, and they are invited to come by the local politicians who do what they can by way of inducements. Why then, should businesspeople worry about taking advantage of these opportunities when they find them? The reason lies in the new broader and *global accountability* the stakeholders expect and demand of corporations. Putting it simply, influential stakeholder groups have made it very difficult for corporations caught offending their values anywhere in the world. The most obvious examples relate to the clothing, sports gear, and toy industries. Major retailers and manufacturers have been compelled by public pressure to ensure that abusive labour practices that have occurred in the past have been eliminated. This is so even when the company had been previously unaware of the abuses.

The growth of the internet in recent years has made it virtually impossible for any multinational to isolate or keep secret knowledge of local conditions to the local communities. If an abuse is occurring, and a company has no processes for discovering it, the risk is that they will first hear about it over the internet at the same time as thousands of others, and not be able to prevent or minimize resulting damage.

In addition, environmental and personal disasters such as at Bhopal, caused by Union Carbide's poorly maintained plant, and in Ecuador, caused by oil spills from a pipeline built by Texaco, have resulted in lawsuits launched or endorsed by the same foreign governments that invited the companies in, and even entreated them to stay in adverse circumstances. In addition, in response to such disasters, lawsuits have also arisen in the jurisdictions where the offending company's stock has been traded because of investors' claims that management was negligent and should have issued warnings of heightened risk caused by reduced safeguards. While it seems that some customers want cheap goods and some investors rejoice in high profits, there are others who care about how these are produced, or are willing to sue if an opportunity presents itself.[2]

More important than the costs of a trial in terms of time lost, and fines, and legal fees paid, companies should realize that the damage to their reputation is usually the largest impact they suffer. The impact of lost reputation may not be seen for some time, but there is no doubt that it can translate into lost future revenues of very large magnitude.

Finally, there is an impact on the morale of domestic employees to be considered from engaging in practices not considered worthy. Their desire to be productive, and to produce at high levels of quality may be undermined, with serious consequences.

Child and Sweatshop Labour Issues

Companies that manufacture in developing countries, or purchase product from such countries, will inevitably run into the issue of use of child labour or of so-called sweatshop labour, especially if they are retailers. This issue has immense ethical implications for producers, retailers, and consumers alike, and there is no easy answer. Ethical models as set out in this book will not provide ready answers, or answers at all. However, they may help a particular company at least consider the most important aspects of the issue so they can demonstrate that they are operating on a duly considered and ethical platform, even if others may disagree with it. Unfortunately, the issue is so intertwined with the emotional views of various NGOs with particular agendas, media attempts to overdramatize particular aspects of the issue, political, and union pressure to preserve jobs locally, and pure xenophobia, that making a sound ethical decision may not be the right thing to do to protect the interests of stakeholders. Whatever approach is taken will likely subject the company to criticism from some quarters, which might cause some companies to take the easy way out and simply go out of business. Nevertheless, the worst possible approach for companies in this situation is to ignore the issue and hope that problems will not occur. This is unethical, because there are important ethical issues at stake, and potentially disastrous for business.

There are a huge number of organizations that operate in this field. Most of them have strong views. All of them base their views on ethical principles. They mostly come up with different, even conflicting, approaches. So what is a company to make of all this? How should its decisions be made? What principles should apply?

---

2. See Texaco's website at: http://www.texaco.com/sitelets/ecuador/en/

To highlight the fundamentally contradictory ethical issues that can arise consider the following:

- A company may decide that, to compete and survive, it must move some of its manufacturing operations offshore to a low-wage country. One of the key issues likely to be raised by existing employees, and local communities, is that it is unethical to fire the existing employees, or to fail to provide new employment opportunities. On the other hand, a moral argument can be made that workers in developing countries need the jobs more than workers in North America, where there is more of a social safety net.
- Using cheap labour permits consumers to benefit from low prices, and most consumers would not willingly forego their bargains for the sake of employing local people. On the other hand, laid off or otherwise unemployed local people do not have the economic wherewithal to pay even the cheaper prices, so the companies will lose business. As with all things, a balance is needed.[3]
- While most people will agree that child labour is immoral, the actual morality is highly complex. If the alternative to child labour is, in practical terms, total destitution, or enticement of children into the sex trades, child labour may be preferable to the alternatives, provided it is not abusive or unsafe. Unduly sanctimonious refusal to contemplate child labour for, say, twelve-year-olds can lead to legitimate arguments that we in the west allow child labour, for example on farms where family members work the harvest, or summer camps where some counsellors are under age. On the other hand, one can argue that children should be in school, not working at full-time jobs.

The remainder of this section deals with sweatshop labour. Child labour is dealt with as a separate issue at the end.

Some principles follow that may be applied when considering taking advantage of low wages paid in developing countries. The key is to consider all stakeholders.

---

3. An interesting example of this conundrum took place recently in Toronto, where the City Council awarded its order for new street cars to a Canadian company that would build them locally, thus providing employment, tax revenue for the government and all kinds of other spin off benefits that would not occur should the contract have been put up for tender and won by a foreign company that had expressed a strong interest. On the other hand, some noted that the Canadian company itself would be devastated if cities in other countries took the same approach, since the company is a major supplier of transportation equipment to foreign countries.

- Why are we manufacturing or purchasing in a low-wage country? Is it necessary for survival? Is it from a genuine belief that quality will improve and benefits will accrue to workers in those countries, and to the countries themselves? Or is it simply to gain a competitive advantage over other companies that employ locally? All may be acceptable, but should be consciously decided and supported.
- Are we treating existing employees fairly if any are to be laid off? Has there been appropriate consultation, alternatives offered, for example pay cuts, compensation established, and help finding new employment provided?
- If there are lay offs, has the effect on the community been considered, and dealt with as fairly as possible?
- Are we paying at least a living wage? A living wage is defined by the International Labour Organization (ILO)[4] to be sufficient to provide one half of what is needed to provide basic housing with indoor plumbing. ready access to clean water, education for children, adequate nutrition, heat in non-tropical countries, preventive health care, and a small percentage for discretionary expenditure. This will obviously vary significantly from one location to another, but the information will usually be locally available from official or unofficial sources.
- Are employees treated on a non-discriminatory basis? For example, are pregnant women treated fairly and given appropriate pregnancy and maternity leave with the right to return to work?
- Are working conditions safe?
- Are reasonable facilities provided, when needed, for accommodation, child care, training, education, and meals, all at reasonable and affordable prices?
- Is there a system in place whereby serious employee abuse can be reported without fear of intimidation?
- Are the conditions actively monitored on a regular basis by organizations or people who are free from bias, and competent to detect abuses? Employees are sometimes intimidated to not report abuses. There are several organizations that perform audits of operations for these purposes.[5]
- Is environmental damage minimized?

---

4. See http://www.ilo.org/public/english/bureau/stat/download/articles/1997–3.pdf
5. See for example, Social Accountability International (SAI) at http://www.sa-intl.org/

Additional considerations apply when a company finds that its subsidiary, partner, or supplier employs child labour, or plans to do so.

- Is the employment of child labour the norm in that location? It is particularly problematical if child labour is illegal but universally tolerated.
- What would be the result on the children, their families, and their communities if child labour were to be immediately terminated? If the damage would be significant, are there means of ending child labour over a period of time without such damaging results?

And if child labour is to be used on a temporary or permanent basis:

- Are working hours sufficient that the children have time to attend school? Better still, can the company provide education for its workers?
- Are the physical aspects of the work unduly onerous for children?
- Is the minimum age reasonable? Five years old, for example, is not reasonable under any circumstances. There is no consensus on an acceptable minimum age, even by those who believe child labour is never justified.
- Do the children have adequate family time? This means travel time between home and work must be considered.

Overall, operating in low-wage countries and employing child labour is fraught with many pitfalls and will inevitably upset some stakeholders. This does not mean that companies should not do it. Economic necessity may make it necessary or desirable. It is critical for the company to consider all its options, and demonstrate that it has considered all the ethical implications and truly believes that on balance it is doing good in the process, and no egregious harm.

Bribery and facilitating payments

In their foreign operations, multinational corporations are likely to be asked for facilitating payments or bribes. A facilitating payment is usually nominal in value and made to speed up a result that would have happened anyway given enough time, for example, a small payment made to customs officials that all importers pay to facilitate movement of goods, such payment usually provides no competitive advantage. A bribe is usually larger than nominal, usually paid to gain a competitive advantage, and without which the desired result would not occur. Both payments are intended to influence outcomes, but some observers believe that a facilitating payment is of lesser ethical consequence than a bribe. Others do not make this distinction.

Most business leaders understand that there is nowhere in the world where bribing government officials is legal in the country where the bribe is paid. Yet at the same time they know that bribery is the normal way of doing business in some regions, and the laws are enforced only sporadically, or not at all. But in all OECD member countries it is now illegal to pay a bribe to a foreign government official. In the United States, the Foreign Corrupt Practices Act is widely known because it has been on the books for many years and is enforced by the SEC, which has imposed serious penalties from time to time. However, there are many who are unaware Canada has an almost exactly identical law called the Corruption of Foreign Public Officials Act[6], passed in 2002, although Canada has been criticized for being lax on enforcement. Basically, senior officials of a Canadian company that caused bribes to be paid to a foreign government official could finish up in jail.

Of course, bribery and corruption is also bad on purely ethical grounds. It can have a devastating affect on development, and creates injustices for those not in a position to benefit, or who have to pay the bribes. It is also damaging to reputations, as was discovered by Acres, a major Canadian engineering consulting firm that was convicted in Lesotho of paying bribes. Even though it had denied guilt, it was forced out of business.

The corporation should have a policy concerning the payment of bribes and facilitating payments, rather than leaving employees to make up their own minds as to when payment is appropriate. For example, it may not be sufficient to simply say that no bribes shall be paid; it is important to provide guidelines to employees concerning what to do if they are asked. If a company permits facilitating payments, it needs to have very strict and clear policies surrounding their payment. The payments should be defined, there should be limits and approval processes, and they should be properly recorded in the accounts.

It should be clear that facilitating payments or bribes are problematic for reasons other than illegality, including:

- Adding to the cost of the operation, good, or service
- Undermining the practice of purchasing based on merit in a country or firm

---

6. Reviewable at http://www.justice.gc.ca/en/dept/pub/cfpoa/guide5.html

- Risking possible negative consequences from stakeholder groups should they find out
- Impossibility of enforcing performance, obtaining a contract, after bribes are paid
- Impossibility of assessing sales force effectiveness
- Indicating to employees elsewhere in the multinational that bribes are permitted in spite of what codes of conduct say
- Indicating to seekers of bribes elsewhere that bribes are possible if they ask for them
- The risk that a change in political control, particularly by revolution, could bring past practices to light, and have serious consequences for the company and personally for local employees involved
- Undermining internal control. Usually, bribes paid are untraceable (e.g., frequently in cash) and management cannot know for sure that the real beneficiary was as reported. The recipient may in fact be an employee of the company who pretended that a bribe needed to be paid.

Some multinationals have banned the giving of bribes or facilitating payments and have continued to operate profitably in the countries concerned. On the other hand, some claim they have lost business to companies who do not have similar scruples. Because of their lower economic power and influence, smaller companies may find it more difficult to resist pressure. The OECD treaty, and resulting legislation helps to level the playing field, but it remains to be seen how helpful this will be to small companies.

The source for extensive and authoritative information on international bribery and corruption is Transparency International (TI), and its Canadian or U.S. branches. Each year, TI publishes its *Corruption Perceptions Index*, which ranks companies based on the perceptions of international business executives and professionals. In its 2007 survey which covered 179 countries, Denmark and Finland were perceived to be the least corrupt nation, and Myanmar the most corrupt, Canada ranked 9th least corrupt, the US 20th, and Mexico 72nd. This index is available on all TI websites. It can be a valuable tool for companies in assessing their operational risks in foreign countries, particularly in countries near the bottom of the list. The following TI websites are gold mines of information and guidance:

http://www.transparency.org – the worldwide site, based in Berlin
http://www.transparency.ca – the Canadian site
http://www.transparency-usa.org – the U.S. site

In some cultures, particularly in Southeastern Asia, China, and Japan, there is a long tradition of gift giving to cultivate long-term relationships that facilitate business dealings. In these situations, corporations may be best advised to have a permissive policy where employees would be required to consult a corporate ethics officer to make sure that cultural niceties are observed without breaking laws at home or abroad. Gift giving might cover such items as a set of golf clubs but would certainly not stretch to a Mercedes.

This is a good example of an issue that has moved from being a business aggravation, to an ethical issue, to a legal issue. But it is still an ethical issue. It needs to be covered in corporate codes of conduct, and business policies and practices when a company is in a position to be asked for a bribe. Policies, especially for decision makers in the field, need to be clear and unequivocal. Canadian or U.S. management will not be saved by ignoring the issue or taking steps to ensure they do not know what goes on locally in high risk countries. In particular, employing an agent to deal with business abroad does not get management off the hook. They are responsible for providing appropriate instructions to agents not to pay bribes, and to monitor their expenditures to be alert for those that might indicate that bribes have been paid. An excellent article on this issue may be found in the October 2006 *CAmagazine* by James Miklotz entitled, "Not Seeing is no Defence" (http://www.camagazine.com/3/3/9/9/2/index1.shtml).

Boards, audit committees, and management of companies operating in high risk parts of the world should expect their auditors to be aware of the associated risk that illegal bribes may have been paid and to take the risk into account in their audits.[7]

Moral Imagination

In some corporations, managers have used their *moral imagination* to devise alternatives that answered needs in the host culture but conformed to North American norms for acceptable behaviour. For example, a manager in China refused to pay an official of a potential customer citing company policy. When the official insisted repeatedly, the manager sought and received approval for a corporate contribution toward the establishment of a community centre in a local park that would offer services to senior citizens. This appealed to Chinese cultural values, allowed them to save face, and was in line with the corporation's North American policy of community support. It was differentiated from a bribe in that no payment was

---

7. This is a requirement of Canadian, U.S. and International auditing standards (CICA Handbook Section 5136, AICPA Au 317 and ISA 250, respectively).

made to an individual for his or her personal benefit, and all payments were made in public rather than in secret.

Guidelines for ethical practice

Two authors have made an extensive study of the ethics of foreign operations, and have written excellent books on the subject. The are Tom Donaldson[8] and Richard DeGeorge[9], and they have each put forward guidelines that may be useful for corporations to take note of. Their views are summarized in an article by Nancy Roth. Tom Donaldson's excellent article on bribery and foreign cultures is also referenced.

Corporations should also compare their values, codes, and practices to the Principles for Business that have been developed for worldwide application by the Caux Round Table in Geneva. These practices are available online at the Caux Round Table's website[10].

Reading *located at the end of the book*

David Selley, "Bribing foreign government officials now illegal," *management ethics* (February 1999): 1–3. Also available online at: http://www.ethicscentre.ca/EN/resources/February%201999%20methics.pdf

Useful References

Richard T. De George, *Competing with Integrity in International Business* (Oxford University Press, 1993).

T. Donaldson, *The Ethics of International Business*, (New York: Oxford University Press, 1989).

T. Donaldson, "Values in Tension: Ethics Away from Home," *Harvard Business Review* Sept.–Oct. (1996): 48–62.

Roth, N. et al, "Can't We All Just Get Along: Cultural Variables in Codes of Ethics," *Public Relations Review* 22 (1996): 151–161.

Transparency International website at http://www.transparency.ca

Additional Readings and Useful References will noted on: http://www.ethicscentre.ca

---

8. Thomas Donaldson, *The Ethics of International Business* (New York: Oxford University Press, 1989).
9. Richard T. De George, *Competing with Integrity in International Business* (Oxford University Press, 1993).
10. http://www.cauxroundtable.org/documents/Principles%20for%20Business.PDF

	Checklist – Special Topics
	International Operations
✓	Do Policies, Codes, Guidelines & Practices consider:
	• Impacts on local economies & their cultures, including:
	○ Labour markets: wage rates, supply
	○ Raw material and other input markets
	○ Political and legal processes
	○ Environmental conditions
	○ Religious and social customs
	• Conflicts between domestic and foreign cultures
	○ Bribery
	○ Use of prison labour
	○ Unhealthy labour conditions
	○ Poor treatment of women
	○ Support of repressive regimes
	○ Lack of respect for the environment
	○ Nepotism
	• Bribery & facilitating payments
	○ Disfunctionality
	○ Undermining of codes, values, and ethics standards
	• Use of moral imagination

Special Topics

Chapter 11
Not-for-profit Entities &
Small Owner-managed Enterprises

Not-for-profit entities

Not-for-profit entities represent a huge segment of our economy. They range from the very large to the very small. These include very large public institutions such as universities, schools and hospitals; large charitable organizations such as the United Way; large non-governmental organizations (NGOs) such as Greenpeace; and small charities and NGOs.

Most of these entities have a number of features in common that make them vulnerable to employee fraud or unethical acts, for example:

- They are usually parsimonious in monetary rewards and benefits to employees, often because they wish to minimize administrative expenses and thereby improve their image. This means that they do not always attract the most competent people into financial management and other responsible positions. Worse still, this parsimony may increase the likelihood that employees will find themselves in financial difficulties and therefore be motivated through need to improve their finances through unethical means.
- In some charities, it is difficult to anticipate incoming donations, thereby making it easier for any diversion of funds to remain unnoticed.
- Boards of Directors may be inadequately compensated, usually they are only reimbursed for expenses, and may be largely comprised of people able to make a financial contribution, rather than those with good oversight skills.
- Need for funding may tempt management to be less than fully honest in applying for government or other grants.

- Stakeholders, in the form of donors, may have even higher expectations than shareholders in profit-oriented enterprises.
- There is usually little or no oversight equivalent to the role market analysts perform for public corporations. Regulation is frequently non-existent or lax.
- Charitable organizations attract very highly principled and committed people. But such people may be so committed to their cause that they may be prepared to step over the line of what is ethical in helping the organization meet its goals.
- Some organizations contract out fund raising without paying adequate attention to the ethical conduct of the organizations they contract out to.

So in all these organizations, tone at the top and a code of conduct are at least as important as in a public corporation, perhaps even more so. Almost everything in this book applies to such organizations. In particular, all but the very smallest organizations should:

- Develop and maintain a code of conduct as set out in this book, insist that all employees act honestly and transparently, and focus on an ethical tone at the top.
- Observe good board of director governance principles, including monitoring of ethical conduct.
- Establish the best possible financial internal controls so as to minimize the temptation for employees, especially those with the ability to intercept incoming funds.
- Insist that two signatures be required on all cheques, and require the second signer to perform due diligence on the payments, see supporting documentation, and so forth. Frequently the second signature is that of the treasurer – a volunteer board member. This is an excellent practice, but only if the treasurer is diligent in understanding what he or she is approving.
- Ensure that compensation and benefits are reasonable for the sector, and be alert for financial distress.
- Maintain scrupulous honesty in grant applications and fund raising activities. If contracted out, insist that fund raisers take an honest and transparent approach, and monitor what they do.
- Be transparent in financial reporting and ensure that annual financial statements are audited. In very large organizations establish an internal audit function.

- In larger organizations consider establishing a whistle-blowing process.

Small owner-managed enterprises

In small owner-managed businesses, the ethical focus of the owner is critical to success. A formal code of conduct may not be necessary, but only if the owner has hands on contact with the entity's day-to-day activities. This provides him or her with the opportunity to convey an ethical tone at the top in both word and deed. This is not a guarantee that unethical conduct or fraud will not occur, but it certainly minimizes the risk. The owner manager needs to demonstrate his or her criteria for ethical treatment of customers and suppliers, employees, as well as all other stakeholders. Note that although small, a small business may nevertheless be the largest employer in its community. Small business owners have certain advantages over public company CEOs because they are not under constant pressure from the market to produce quarterly earnings. Unless under serious financial strain from lenders, the small business owner can afford to take a longer-term view and focus on establishing the reputation of the business for quality, value for money, and most importantly, integrity and fairness to primary stakeholders, particularly customers and employees.

In southwestern Ontario every year a large number of farm workers are imported from Mexico for the summer and fall harvest. These workers are paid minimum wages and work hard. But what they earn is, for them, an opportunity to build a family nest egg that they could not do at home. Many stories have surfaced about the friendly reception these Mexican workers get from the farmers and the community. They are provided with basic but comfortable accommodation, and are treated with dignity. The benefit to the farmers, truly owner-managed businesses, is pervasive. They are perceived to be acting ethically, which is good for their standing in the community, and therefore their business.

But even owner managers need to take some specific steps to ensure that their ethical standards are actually implemented and that fraud is deterred. For example, owner managers should:

- Ensure that employees are aware that honesty is a cornerstone of the business and dishonesty towards customers, suppliers, lenders, and other stakeholders will not be tolerated.
- Approve all significant transactions and review all other transactions after the fact.

- Sign all cheques.
- Obtain bank statements directly from the bank, and review them to ensure they recognize all the content. Every now and then they could perform the bank reconciliation.
- Keep a list of all sales, and cross-check on a regular basis to incoming funds.
- Unless absent, make it a point to talk to all employees at least once per week and to senior employees on a daily basis.
- Ensure that all senior people take vacations.

Owner managers should also be sensitive to the example set by their own conduct. For example, if they habitually charge personal expenses to the company, such as rebuilding their swimming pool, they are not sending a good message to their employees, who will quickly perceive a lack of honesty and may be tempted to imitate when the opportunity arises.

In short, an owner manager will find it significantly easier, with a modicum of diligence, to instill his or her ethical values into the way the business is run. However, to be successful, this requires constant communication and hands on involvement in the day-to-day activities of the business. And of course, any ethical lapse by the owner manager may have an equally negative effect on the conduct of other employees.

Useful References

Business Ethics for SMEs, Business Ethics Briefing, Institute of Business Ethics, December 2007, Issue 6, downloadable from: http://www.ibe.org.uk/BusinessEthicsforSMEs.pdf including other useful readings and websites.

J.J. Quinn, "Personal Ethics and Business Ethics: The Attitudes of Owner/managers of Small Business," *Journal of Business Ethics* 16:2 (1997): 199–127.

L.J. Spence, *Pracitice, Priorities, and Ethics in Small Firms*, (London: Institute of Business Ethics, 2000). Available online at: http://www.ibe.org.uk/PPE.html

Checklist – Special Topics
Not-for-profit Entities & Small Owner-managed Enterprises
✓   Does the organization consider or have
• Exemplary tone at the top
• Code of conduct featuring:
o Honesty
o Transparency
• Training & notification to ensure employees know expectations
• Ethical Governance Principles including monitoring
• Internal controls to remove temptation for employees
• Dual cheque signing with a second knowledgeable signatory performing due diligence
• Prior review of all significant transactions
• Review & reconciliation of Bank Statements
• Review reports for significant transactions
• Monitoring for financial distress of employees
• Scrupulously honest grant or fund raising procedures
• Transparent financial reports
• Audit of financial statements
• Internal audit function if needed
• Whistle-blowing mechanism
• Ongoing contact and chats with employees
• All senior employees must take a vacation

Concluding Comments

Most would agree that reputation is absolutely critical to success in any organization; not only for businesses, but also for not-for-profit organizations of all types. Reputation is earned primarily through the use of quality processes, and the provision of quality products and services at an appropriate price. But it can be destroyed, or at least badly tarnished, by perceived ethical lapses and failure to properly deal with such lapses when they do occur.

There was a day when ethical lapses could be kept hidden. Today this reactive approach to damage control will not work. Bear in mind that almost everyone now has a camera embedded in her or his cell phone. Instant global communications and the growth of the internet and its offshoots such as YouTube mean that what would previously been hidden or given limited circulation may be broadcast almost instantaneously to the whole world. A preventive, forthright approach to the management of ethics risks is more important than ever.

But maintaining the ethical integrity of any organization comprised of human beings with all their frailties and mistakes can be a daunting challenge. It is hard work, requiring constant vigilance and increasing expertise. In response, this book offers practical help to those with primary responsibility for developing and maintaining an ethical culture in their organization, and to upper and middle management personnel who are responsible for implementing it. The book emphasizes that it is a necessary, but not sufficient, condition that the organization's leadership and those charged with its governance behave ethically and communicate the need and expectations for ethical culture to all employees and agents. The culture must be lived every day throughout the organization and must be built-in to all key processes.

To achieve this objective this book provides practical guidance, examples, and readings on the key aspects of developing and maintaining an ethical corporate culture. It covers:

- Understanding what it means to have an ethical culture, to be a good corporate citizen, and to keep the support of stakeholders (Chapter 2)
- How to provide the leadership necessary to instill the culture throughout the organization (Chapter 3)
- How to effectively communicate the organization's culture to those who need to live by it (Chapter 4)
- How to constantly reinforce the culture so that it does not become a "flavour of the month" – a frequent fate of many management initiatives that are not constantly reinforced and do not achieve the necessary buy in from employees (Chapter 6)
- The need to continually monitor actual performance so that process improvements can be identified and successes (and failures) measured (Chapter 7).
- Guidance for leadership and management on how to make good ethical decisions, including some "rules of thumb" and commentary on a range of ethical conceptual frameworks (Chapter 8)
- Guidance on specific topics such as conflicts of interest, so-called "whistle-blowing" processes, ethical international operations (including bribery and corruption issues), and ethics for not-for-profit organizations ranging from large organizations with public accountability such as hospitals, schools and universities, and large and small charitable organizations (Chapters 5 and 9 through 11).

The cliché that business ethics is an oxymoron and the notion that an organization cannot, by its nature, be ethical are now both generally viewed as completely obsolete. Public expectations of all organizations will continue to grow, fueled by insights stimulated by new information and misinformation, and fresh examples of unfortunate as well as exemplary behaviour.

What will the future bring? Today's hot button issues such as concern for the environment, sweatshop and child labour, and unfair competition, will not diminish. New hot button issues will emerge as stakeholder interests are sharpened by new information and by understanding better the potential for successful influence on organizational activities. The price to be paid for failing to anticipate problems or not to meet performance expectations will grow, not diminish. The recent past offers many examples of corporations and individuals who failed tragically, not because they didn't have a great product or service, or because they didn't have a respected governance system, but because they failed to fully embrace a culture of integrity.

This book is dedicated to helping those charged with developing and maintaining an ethical culture in their organization to navigate successfully through the intricacies of making it happen.

Appendix A: CSR & Sustainability Reports, Indexes & Rankings

Evidence of the pervasiveness of stakeholder interest in an organization's practices can be found in the following company lists, indexes, and rankings detailed below, and on the accompanying website at http://www.ethicscentre.ca including:

- 25 companies with recent CSR reports per the GRI website
- 10 companies included in the Jantzi Social Index of October 2007
- 100 companies included in The 2007 AccountAbility Ranking
- 31 companies with CSR reports and related website addresses
- Over 300 companies included in the Dow Jones Sustainability Index World October 2007

25 Companies With Recent CSR Reports Per the GRI website
Company Name
American Electric Power
Barclays plc
BP plc
Canon Inc
Chevron Corporation
Coca-Cola Enterprises Inc.
Disco Corporation
E.ON UK
Fuji Xerox Co Ltd.
GlaxoSmithKline plc
Hess Corporation
Hewlett-Packard Company
Insurance Australia Group Limited
Komatsu Ltd
Marks and Spencer plc
Mitsubishi Corporation
Nationwide Building Society
Nexen Inc.
Nikon Corporation
02 (Telefónica Europe plc)
SABMiller plc
Sony Corporation
Toyota Industries Corporation
Vancouver City Savings Credit Union
Vodafone Group plc

Source: GRI website, http://www.globalreporting.org

Companies in Jantzi Social Index, October 2007	
Company Name	**Sector**
Alcan	Materials
BCE Inc.	Telecommunication
Canadian National Railway	Industrials
Encana	Energy
Biovail Corp	Health Care
Research in Motion	Information Technology
Rogers Communication	Consumer Discretionary
Royal Bank of Canada	Financials
Shoppers Drug Mart	Consumer Staples
Transalta Corp.	Utilities

Reprinted from: Jantzi Social Index website, http://www.jantzisocialindex.com

#	Company Name	Overall score	Strategy	Governance	Engagement	Impact
	Companies in the 2007 AccountAbility Ranking					
1	BP	75.2	82.9	85.4	73.7	58.9
2	Barclays	68.5	81.7	60.7	43.0	88.4
3	ENI	67.9	75.6	57.8	50.5	87.5
4	HSBC Holdings	67.2	93.0	66.4	59.5	50.0
5	Vodafone	66.3	88.1	70.9	81.9	24.6
6	Royal Dutch/Shell Group	66.0	81.2	78.9	68.1	35.7
7	Peugeot	63.7	85.4	65.9	28.6	75.0
8	HBOS	62.0	76.0	71.7	56.4	43.8
9	Chevron	61.6	64.2	55.2	39.5	87.5
10	DaimlerChrysler	60.1	81.6	66.6	48.5	43.8
11	Tesco	60.0	65.6	62.9	49.0	62.5
12	BASF	59.8	69.8	58.0	46.4	65.2
13	General Electric	59.1	67.9	53.9	26.1	88.4
14	ABN Amro	57.6	85.4	52.9	35.8	56.3
15	ING Group	56.9	78.4	59.9	50.9	38.4
16	E.ON	56.5	78.0	58.1	52.6	37.5
17	Statoil	56.1	66.2	61.9	34.0	62.5
18	Total	55.1	62.8	65.7	50.0	42.0
19	Repsol YPF	54.3	63.8	56.4	53.1	43.8
20	Électricité de France	54.3	82.3	47.3	50.0	37.5
21	Marathon Oil	54.2	52.9	45.3	31.1	87.5
22	General Motors	53.4	81.7	65.3	25.6	41.1
23	Telefónica	52.9	76.4	58.3	46.9	29.9
24	HP	52.6	84.7	54.5	40.1	31.3
25	Nestlé	51.7	73.6	52.4	27.2	53.6
26	Carrefour	50.1	77.7	48.9	30.2	43.8
27	Ford Motor	50.0	77.7	57.1	27.6	37.5
28	Petróleo Brasileiro SA	49.8	63.5	46.1	45.7	43.8
29	Matsushita Electric Industrial	49.7	57.4	39.5	27.1	75.0
30	Toshiba	49.6	70.8	46.2	43.8	37.5
31	Procter & Gamble	49.1	58.2	40.6	22.7	75.0
32	Citigroup	48.6	61.2	54.0	23.1	56.3
33	Deutsche Telekom	46.7	62.2	26.9	19.5	78.1
34	Sony	46.4	53.6	30.8	23.1	78.1
35	Aviva	45.8	69.6	49.0	27.1	37.5
36	Fortis	44.5	72.7	34.9	33.0	37.5

#	Company Name	Overall score	Strategy	Governance	Engagement	Impact
	Companies in the 2007 AccountAbility Ranking					
37	Royal Bank of Scotland	44.0	62.1	43.0	27.3	43.8
38	Toyota Motor	44.0	68.1	45.2	30.4	32.1
39	Volkswagen	43.8	79.2	36.8	32.6	26.8
40	Société Générale	43.3	62.3	33.2	33.9	43.8
41	Siemens	42.7	68.5	35.6	22.9	43.8
42	Dexia	42.5	66.4	51.6	25.1	26.8
43	AXA	41.9	70.9	36.8	22.3	37.5
44	SK Energy (SK Holdings)	41.8	44.6	31.9	53.4	37.5
45	Fiat	41.8	55.0	38.1	30.4	43.8
46	France Telecom	41.5	68.7	31.9	30.4	35.3
47	BMW	41.0	72.4	30.8	17.1	43.8
48	Exxon Mobil	40.3	49.2	35.0	27.0	50.0
49	UniCredit Group	39.9	54.4	27.9	39.8	37.5
50	Santander	39.4	55.9	26.0	38.3	37.5
51	ConocoPhillips	39.4	49.0	46.6	22.6	39.3
52	IBM	39.1	61.3	36.0	19.9	39.3
53	Credit Suisse	39.0	63.2	40.8	18.9	33.0
54	Deutsche Bank	38.4	65.1	44.6	17.3	26.8
55	Crédit Agricole	37.6	58.1	37.7	17.1	37.5
56	Hyundai Motor	37.5	60.9	28.5	28.7	32.1
57	Sinopec	36.2	53.0	26.6	27.8	37.5
58	LG	36.2	36.8	36.8	33.7	37.5
59	BNP Paribas	36.1	62.9	27.6	27.0	26.8
60	UBS	35.8	54.6	44.6	11.9	32.1
61	Prudential	35.7	42.6	49.4	13.3	37.5
62	Honda Motor	35.3	52.9	26.6	24.2	37.5
63	Samsung Electronics	35.3	53.3	36.9	24.1	26.8
64	Deutsche Post	34.7	58.2	20.6	22.5	37.5
65	Allianz	34.5	52.4	32.3	15.7	37.5
66	Nissan Motor	33.2	52.5	24.4	18.4	37.5
67	JPMorgan Chase	31.6	39.2	33.3	10.3	43.8
68	Bank of America Corp.	31.6	44.7	27.5	10.6	43.8
69	State Grid	31.0	52.3	15.1	19.1	37.5
70	Hitachi	30.3	33.0	29.5	21.2	37.5
71	Assicurazioni Generali	29.6	38.3	25.8	16.8	37.5
72	Munich RE	29.3	48.2	20.9	10.7	37.5

#	Company Name	Overall score	Strategy	Governance	Engagement	Impact
	Companies in the 2007 AccountAbility Ranking					
76	Goldman Sachs Group	27.9	36.3	27.8	10.2	37.5
77	Nippon Telegraph & Telephone	27.7	32.8	26.7	13.7	37.5
78	Metro	27.2	49.6	13.2	8.6	37.5
79	Morgan Stanley	26.3	35.3	34.4	2.6	33.0
80	China National Petroleum	26.0	36.0	14.0	16.6	37.5
81	Home Depot	25.3	51.7	19.8	8.2	21.4
82	Zurich Financial Services	25.1	36.1	18.1	8.9	37.5
83	Target	24.1	19.8	28.8	10.4	37.5
84	American Intl. Group	22.7	40.8	28.6	8.9	12.5
85	US Postal Service	21.9	27.1	15.8	7.4	37.5
86	Gazprom	21.8	20.4	22.3	12.4	32.1
87	Wal-Mart Stores	20.3	28.9	23.0	11.4	17.9
88	McKesson	19.7	22.2	12.0	7.1	37.5
89	Boeing	19.3	18.8	19.3	1.8	37.5
90	Kroger	19.0	15.7	15.7	7.3	37.5
91	Pemex	18.5	16.8	5.9	13.9	37.5
92	UnitedHealth Group	16.8	20.0	27.1	3.8	16.1
93	AT&T	16.7	10.2	18.2	6.2	32.1
94	AmerisourceBergen	16.7	10.4	14.5	4.3	37.5
95	Valero Energy	14.8	10.0	15.1	2.0	32.1
96	ArcelorMittal	14.2	22.3	19.2	4.7	10.7
97	Cardinal Health	13.7	13.4	14.9	5.1	21.4
98	State Farm Insurance Cos.	12.8	6.4	2.8	4.6	37.5
99	Berkshire Hathaway	10.1	4.0	4.3	0.0	32.1
100	Costco Wholesale	8.9	3.3	8.6	2.4	21.4

Reprinted from: AccountAbility Ranking website, http://www.accountability21.net

Examples of Corporate Social Responsibility Reports	
Company Name	
Alcan Rio Tinto	http://www.riotinto.com/investors/ 219_sustainable_development.asp
American Electric Power	http://www.aep.com/citizenship/crreport/
Barclays plc	http://www.personal.barclays.co.uk/BRC1/jsp/ brccontrol?site=pfs&task=channelFWsocial&value=9894
BP plc	http://www.bp.com/ subsection.do?categoryId=6845&contentId=7021544
Canadian National Railway	http://www.cn.ca/about/delivering_responsibly/ en_delivering_responsibly.shtml
Canon Inc	http://www.canon.com/scsa/index.html
Chevron Corporation	http://www.chevron.com/globalissues/corporateresponsibility/ 2006/
Coca-Cola Enterprises Inc	http://www.cokecce.com/pages/allContent.asp?page_id=72
Disco Corporation	http://www.discousa.com/eg/corporate/report/index.html
Dofasco	http://www.dofasco.ca/bins/content_page.asp?cid=339–340
Enbridge Inc	http://www.enbridge.com/corporate/
Encana	http://www.encana.com/responsibility/reporting/index.htm
Exxon Mobil Corporation	http://www.exxonmobil.com/Corporate/community.aspx
Fuji Xerox Co Ltd	http://www.fujixerox.co.jp/eng/social/index.html
GlaxoSmithKline plc	http://www.gsk.com/reportsandpublications.htm
Hess Corporation	http://www.hess.com/ehs/env_health_safety.htm
Hewlett-Packard Company	http://www.hp.com/hpinfo/globalcitizenship/
Insurance Australia Group Limited	http://www.iag.com.au/sustainable/reports/index.shtml
Komatsu Ltd	http://www.komatsu.com/CompanyInfo/csr/
Marks and Spencer plc	http://www.marksandspencer.com/gp/node/n/ 43451031?ie=UTF8&mnSBrand=core
Mountain Equipment Co-op	http://www.mec.ca/Main/content_text.jsp?FOLDER%3C% 3Efolder_id=1408474396038945&FOLDER%3C%3EbrowsePath=14 08474396038945&bmUID=1195865967725
Nationwide Building Society	http://www.nationwide.co.uk/bettersociety/tools/printable.htm
Nexen Inc	http://www.nexeninc.com/Sustainability/Sustainability_Report/
Nikon Corporation	http://www.nikon.co.jp/main/eng/portfolio/csr/index.htm

02 (Telefónica Europe plc)	http://www.02.com/reporting_our_activity.asp
Royal Bank of Canada	http://www.rbc.com/responsibility/index.html
SABMiller plc	http://www.sabmiller.com/sabmiller.com/en_gb/Our+responsibility/
Toyota Industries Corporation	http://www.toyota.com/about/our_commitment/index.html
Transalta Corp.	http://www.transalta.com/transalta/webcms.nsf/AllDoc/CEE3B9AC0C40DC6B87257157004FB037?OpenDocument
Vancouver City Savings Credit Union	https://www.vancity.com/MyMoney/AboutUs/WhoWeAre/CorporateReports/AccountabilityReport/
Vodafone Group plc	http://www.vodafone.com/start/responsibility/publications_faqs.html

This list of companies issuing CSR Reports is drawn from the websites listed elsewhere in Appendix A plus that for *The Corporate Knights Magazine* at http://www.corporateknights.ca/reports/

Companies in Dow Jones Sustainability Index, World, October 2007
Company, Country, Industry
3i Group plc, United Kingdom, Financials
3M Co., United States, Industrials
ABB Ltd., Switzerland, Industrials
Abbott Laboratories, United States, Health Care
Abertis Infraestructuras, S.A. Spain, Industrials
ABN AMRO Holding N.V., Netherlands, Financials
Acciona S.A., Spain, Industrials
Accor S.A., France, Consumer Services
Actividades de Construccion y Servicios S.A., Spain, Industrials
adidas AG, Germany, Consumer Goods
Advanced Micro Devices Inc., United States, Technology
Aegon N.V., Netherlands, Financials
Aeon Co. Ltd., Japan, Consumer Services
Agilent Technologies Inc., United States, Industrial Goods & Services
AGL Energy Ltd., Australia, Utilities
Air France-KLM, France, Consumer Services
Akzo Nobel N.V., Netherlands, Basic Materials
Alcatel-Lucent, France, Technology
Alcoa Inc., United States, Basic Materials
Allianz SE, Germany, Financials
AMEC plc, United Kingdom, Industrials
Amgen Inc., United States, Health Care
AMP Ltd., Australia, Financials
Anglo American plc, United Kingdom, Basic Materials
Aracruz Celulose S/A Pref B, Brazil, Basic Materials
Asahi Breweries Ltd., Japan, Consumer Goods
Asahi Glass Co. Ltd., Japan, Industrials
ASML Holding N.V., Netherlands, Technology
Astrazeneca plc, United Kingdom, Health Care
ASX Ltd., Australia, Financials
Atlas Copco AB Series A, Sweden, Industrials
Australia and New Zealand Banking Group Ltd., Australia, Financials
Aviva plc, United Kingdom, Financials
AXA S.A., France, Financials
BAE Systems plc, United Kingdom, Industrials
Balfour Beatty plc, United Kingdom, Industrials
Baloise-Holding AG, Switzerland, Financials
For remaining 280+ companies, see http://www.sustainability-indexes.com/djsi_pdf/

Source: Dow Jones Sustainability World Index (DJSI) website,
http://www.sustainability-index.com

Appendix B: Governance Framework Requirements

Governance Framework

The objective of a governance framework is to ensure that an organization's activities, through the actions of its employees and agents, are in the best interests of its stakeholders. According to past practice, boards of directors have overseen the corporation on behalf of the owners to make sure activities were in the best interest of the company, of the shareholders, really, and the board was expected to institute such governance mechanisms as they needed to ensure that the company optimally achieved its strategic objectives. Without appropriate governance mechanisms – suitable strategies, guidance through an ethical culture, encouragement, monitoring, reporting, rewards, and penalties – employees and agents could engage in suboptimal activities such as putting their interests ahead of the organization's, or placing the organization's reputation at significant risk.

Relatively recently, during the 1990s, corporate accountability expanded to include a broader set of stakeholders. In 1994 and 1995, pronouncements from the Toronto Stock Exchange (now the TSX) and the CICA introduced the thinking that boards of directors were required to foster an ethical corporate culture. Recognizing this, at around the same time some major public accounting firms incorporated stakeholder risk analysis into their audit methodologies as a means of identifying their clients' business risks, and therefore their own audit risks.

The role of the board and its relationships with other actors in the governance framework are portrayed in Figure 1.

In general terms, the board of directors is expected to further the prospects of the company through:

**Figure 1 Appendix B
Corporate Governance Framework**

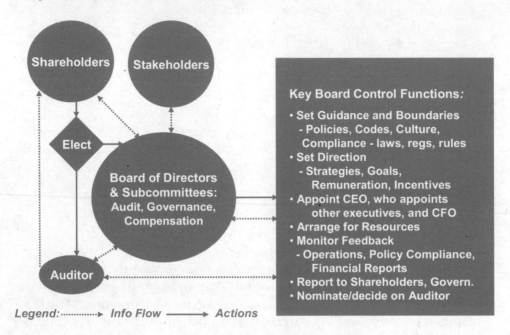

- Oversight – setting or approving strategies and processes, monitoring actions, and improving them or correcting errors
- Ensuring appropriate strategies & objectives reflect values, ethics, competitive advantage, and risk assessment; meet challenges and stakeholder expectations; and incorporate both long- and short-term time horizons
- Ensuring appropriate actions by:
  - Appointing & monitoring CEO, CFO performance
  - Promoting ethical leadership – values and tone at the top
  - Creating and approving ethical guidance – culture, code and rules, learning, encouragement, decision making, internal controls, monitoring mechanisms, enforcement, feedback,
  - Providing adequate resources
  - Monitoring compliance with laws, rules and regulations
- Reporting to stakeholders for support incorporating
  - Transparency, integrity, comprehensiveness
- Nominating the auditor

The board's responsibility can best be achieved by developing and maintaining an ethical corporate culture. In fact, directors and senior officers are legally responsible for the creation and maintenance of a system that ensures that employees act ethically, and the quality of that effort has become a criterion for the establishment of a "due diligence" defence that would relieve a corporate director from legal liability for the misdeeds of employees. In its 1994 *Report of the Toronto Stock Exchange Committee on Corporate Governance in Canada*, the TSE (now TSX) stated that directors have a responsibility to ensure that an ethical culture exists in an organization[1]. The Canadian Institute of Chartered Accountants followed in 1995 by setting out the appropriate criteria for control of a corporation. Specifically, they identified an organization's ethical culture as a fundamental element of its internal control[2]. For example, *Guidance on Control* issued by The Canadian Institute of Chartered Accountants (CICA) states:

> Shared ethical values influence all behaviour in an organization. Together with an understanding of mission and vision, they constitute the basic identity that will shape the way an individual, group, organization or board will operate, and they provide stability over time. Shared values contribute to control because they provide a guide for individual, group or team decision-making, action and policy.[3]

Similar developments in the U.S. have focused on how the directors have put systems into place to ensure that ethical and operational problems do not occur. The U.S. *Sarbanes-Oxley Act of 2002*[4], for example, was enacted to reform corporate governance and disclosure in an effort to restore credibility eroded by Enron and other corporate scandals, and facilitate capital markets that rely on the trust that shareholders, and the public interest, will not be misled and subverted. In response, governance regulations have been revised to some extent around the world.

Consequences can be severe under the *1991 U.S. Sentencing Guidelines*, unless the "due diligence" protection is available. Legal cases like *Caremark National Inc.* (1996)[5] have reinforced the need for directors to maintain information systems that monitor ethical performance, and proactively

---

1. *Report of the Toronto Stock Exchange Committee on Corporate Governance in Canada*, December 1994, paragraphs 4.3 and 4.4.
2. *Guidance for Directors – Governance Processes for Control* (Toronto: Canadian Institute of Chartered Accountants, December 1995), page 2, paragraph 8. See also pages 8 & 9 for a discussion of approving and monitoring the organization's ethical values.
3. *Guidance on Control* (Canadian Institute of Chartered Accountants, November 1995), paragraph 59.
4. Downloadable from http://www.thomsonedu.com/accounting/brooks
5. See Law Case Summary at the end of this appendix.

seek out and rectify causes of ethical problems. The Report of the Toronto Stock Exchange Committee on Corporate Governance in Canada made this point very well:

> Having said that directors have no corporate law duty to act in the best inter-est of any particular stakeholder group [*other than shareholders*], it is obvious that a board cannot make decisions without understanding the implications of its decision for this broader group of stakeholders. In making decisions to enhance shareholder value the board must take into account the interests of other stakeholders. In today's environment it is difficult for a corporation to prosper if it is not "on side" with all its stakeholders.[6]
> (*Italics added*)

Decisions integrating shareholder and stakeholder interests are not as difficult as previously thought. They can be made using stakeholder impact analysis and philosophical techniques that are discussed in Chapter 8.

Directors wishing to be up-to-date would be well advised to join an organization such as the Institute for Corporate Directors (ICD), which has developed an education and certification process (ICD.D), and provides information through its website at http://www.icd.ca, or the NACD (National Association of Corporate Directors), and refer to its website at http://www.nacdonline.org/nacd/governance.asp.

Regulation of ethical conduct

Of course, many things that are unethical are illegal, and corporations, whether private or public, have to follow the law. As emphasized by Lynn Sharp Paine, merely following the law is not sufficient to satisfy stakehold-ers, and maintain the integrity and reputation of a business. Corporations are subject to many kinds of rules and regulations concerning such matters as employee health and safety, product safety, environmental performance, and various forms of licensing. Public companies in most of the world are also subject to a vast array of detailed regulations concerning governance, insider trading, and financial reporting rules that in a large entity require an army of people to administer. The scope of these regulations expanded as a result of corporate financial scandals that came to light in the 1980s, and continues to do so. More and more regulatory pieces have come into play.

---

6. "Where Were The Directors? Guidelines for Improved Corporate Governance in Canada," *Report of the Toronto Stock Exchange Committee on Corporate Governance in Canada* (Toronto: December 1994): Section 4.17, p. 21.

Financial Regulation

Financial regulatory initiatives that apply to public companies in North America aimed at shareholder protection include the following:

- Regulations of stock exchanges and securities commissions that require companies to publicly disclose compliance with corporate governance criteria, and in Canada, the audit committee charter.
- *Sarbanes-Oxley Act* (SOX) in the U.S., and equivalent securities polices in Canada that are in the process of being implemented
- The establishment of bodies to oversee the performance of auditors in Canada and the U.S., as well as other countries worldwide.

All these rules and regulations have an ethical base, although they may not usually be considered in that light. Dealing with a bureaucrat about an arcane regulation relating to the applicability of an insider trading rule is not usually considered to be an exercise in applied ethics, and understandably so. But in recent years, in response to highly publicized ethical and legal lapses by large corporations, the United States Congress has reacted with legislation, and other countries, including Canada, have followed. This legislation has primarily focussed on the particular interests of investors and shareholders, who were cheated out of millions of dollars. As an aside, it is interesting to note that legislators and regulators do not seem to be nearly as concerned about protecting the interests of other stakeholders who lost millions, such as employees.

Details of regulatory requirements outlined in this appendix may be found on the websites of the relevant regulatory body. In North America these would include:

- U.S.A.
  - SEC http://www.sec.gov
  - PCAOB http://www.pcaobus.org/
  - NYSE http://www.nyse.com
- Canada
  - CSA http://www.csa-acvm.ca/
  - CPAB http://www.cpab-ccrc.ca
  - Ontario Securities Commission (OSC) http://www.osc.gov.on.ca/
  - TSX http://www.tsx.com/

Guidance on the application of these regulations may also be found in publications of law and accounting firms. These are usually more user friendly for non-experts.

A useful example of modern governance can be found in the Rogers Governance Report which is available online at http://www.shoprogers. com/corporategovernance/corporategovernance_ overview.asp.

Toronto Stock Exchange governance disclosure requirements

Larger Canadian public companies are required to file an Annual Information Form (AIF) that, among other things, requires companies to append their audit committee's charter and to state whether they have complied with certain recommended (and voluntary) corporate governance criteria.

Sarbanes-Oxley Act (SOX) and Canadian equivalents

In 2002 the U.S. Congress passed the *Sarbanes-Oxley Act*. The important thing about this legislation is that it focussed directly on ethical conduct by senior management, and others such as boards of directors and audit committees, who have management oversight responsibilities. While this legislation is primarily related to honesty in financial reporting, and the U.S. Securities and Exchange Commission (SEC) was given responsibility for applying the act, its effect is much broader. For example, the audit committee is held responsible for monitoring complaints from employees about the honesty of management in relation to financial reporting.

The primary aspects of the SOX legislation and resulting regulation are:

- A requirement that public companies evaluate and disclose the effectiveness of their internal controls as they relate to financial reporting, and that independent auditors for such companies "attest" (i.e., agree, or not) to such disclosure and express an opinion on the adequacy of internal controls as they relate to financial reporting. For smaller entities and foreign issuers, the attest requirements are not yet in force, and some aspects are still subject to discussion.
- Certification of financial reports by chief executive officers and chief financial officers. Criminal liability can attach for knowingly certifying inaccurate reports.
- Auditor independence, including outright bans on certain types of work for audit clients and pre-certification by the company's audit committee of all audit and non-audit work.
- A requirement that companies listed on stock exchanges have fully independent audit committees that oversee the relationship between the company and its auditor.
- A ban on most personal loans to any executive officer or director.

- Employee protections allowing those corporate fraud whistle-blowers who file complaints within ninety days of termination or other disciplinary action to win reinstatement, back pay and benefits, compensatory damages, and costs.

Similar requirements are now, or soon will be, part of Canadian securities regulation except that the Canadian Securities Administrators (CSA) have announced that they do not intend to require auditor attestation of management's report on its internal controls. The independence requirements for auditors were established by the Canadian accounting profession, rather than securities regulators, and are in some respects more rigorous than those of the SEC.

For reasons of lack of space, and because they are constantly changing, it is not the purpose of this publication to provide guidance on compliance with securities regulation in North America. Guidance on these matters is readily available from the regulators themselves, with much needed interpretive guidance from accounting firms and law firms. Rather, our purpose is to emphasize how legislators and regulators are moving into ethical behavioural issues.

For example, both the SOX and Canadian regulations require companies to report on the adequacy of their internal controls over financial reporting, using the so-called COSO[7] criteria. One of the most important of these criteria is "tone at the top," which emphasizes the importance of demonstrably ethical behaviour by CEOs and other senior officers. COSO's criteria also specifically emphasizes that business ethics represents an important element of the risk management process.

Both the U.S. and Canada have many other regulatory bodies that influence financial reporting and auditing in specific industries, especially those relating to the provision of financial services.

Oversight of the public accounting profession

Failure of auditors to catch some of the accounting frauds of the eighties and nineties had ethical dimensions, and led to tougher auditing and independence standards in North America, and internationally.

---

7. Committee of Sponsoring Organizations of the Treadway Commission (COSO) http://www.sox-online.com/coso_cobit_coso.html is a voluntary private sector organization dedicated to improving the quality of financial reporting through business ethics, effective internal controls, and corporate governance. It arose in response to serious financial reporting frauds that had occurred in the 1980s. In 1992 COSO developed a framework and criteria for reporting on internal controls that had become widely accepted in the U.S. prior to the SOX legislation. Although a somewhat different framework was developed in Canada, the COSO framework now appears to have become universal.

The Public Company Accounting Oversight Board (PCAOB) was created by the SOX legislation in the United States, and reports to the SEC. One of its mandates is to oversee and inspect the performance of audits of public companies. All firms that perform such audits are required to register with PCAOB; large firms are inspected annually and smaller ones less frequently. The inspections are rigorous and failure to comply with recommendations and requirements of PCAOB can result in drastic penalties.

PCAOB's equivalent in Canada is the Canadian Public Accountability Board (CPAB), which conducts similar inspections of audit firms that audit public companies. Its power stems from a requirement of the Canadian Securities Administrators (CSA) that will not accept from registrant companies a report from an auditor that is not in good standing with CPAB.

Both PCAOB and CPAB are independent of the public accounting profession. Both bodies focus on more than just technical compliance with auditing, accounting, and independence rules. They consider a firm's quality controls, particularly those relating to the need for emphasis on audit quality and independence, including "tone at the top."

Non-financial Regulation

Most companies are affected by laws and regulations related to their particular business. The focus of many of these requirements is fundamentally ethical, whether it be public or employee safety, or environmental in nature. In almost all cases, if a company runs afoul of such requirements, it incurs not only legal penalties but reputational damage, occasionally of a catastrophic nature. In fact, even if not penalized under law, the revelations involved may still damage reputations.

Summary

The fact that legislators and regulators are moving further into the business ethics field should not lead to complacency or a belief following the rules is enough to stay out of trouble. Far from it. Regulations tend to focus on form, sometimes at the expense of substance. Governance processes and internal control structures will work well only if those responsible for implementing them act in an ethical manner. When it comes to audit committees, for example, it appears that Enron had all the right structures in place. Indeed, some have said the audit committee's mandate was exemplary. However, the process failed because the people who were involved were not as diligent as they should have been. Diligence in matters ethical is a business imperative, whether there are rules or not.

Readings

Len Brooks, "Sniff Tests," *Corporate Ethics Monitor,* **7:5 (1995): 65.**

Sniff Tests

How many times have you wished there were a few key questions you or your employees could ask about an activity to assess quickly whether it is ethical, or whether further ethical study is needed? How many executives wish their employees had asked such quick but fundamental questions before taking an action that ultimately turned out to be very embarrassing for them and damaging for their organization? Why not head off such problems by developing tests for your organization to use to clarify whether an action is ethical or unethical, to sniff out unethical activities before they become troublesome, and to identify when and how an activity should be changed to make it ethical.

Sniff tests can focus the attention of decision makers on the impact of the activity or option on the organization's stakeholders, including the decision maker. For instance, to test whether the activity is fair, the decision maker could ask: *Would I regard this as fair if this were done to me?* A follow-up question that addresses remedial concerns could be: *How would I want the activity changed if I were the focus of it?*

Ethical decision making does not always make everyone happy. But to test whether the activity is right, a sniff test might be: *Is it legal?* But this is not a strong enough test on its own because there are many activities that are legal but not ethical. Some sniff-test questions that may be useful here are: *What would the public think of this activity if the reasons behind the decision were on TV or the front page of tomorrow's newspaper? or What would my children think of this?* or the acid test, *What would my mother think of this?*

There are often trade-offs to be made between various stakeholders because few activities are good for everyone. Trade-offs can be raised and assessed by the following chain of questions: *Does every stakeholder benefit from this activity? Is the harm caused to one or more of the parties offset by the benefits created for others? Is there any harm being created that is permanent or contrary to organizational guidelines? After looking at all potential benefits and harm caused in the next 10 years, is the net benefit marginal? Should I consult my superiors about the risk inherent in this activity?*

Ethical problems tend to become much worse over time than most decision makers expect. Consequently, sniff tests that probe the future are useful, such as: *What's the worst-case ethical scenario that could result from this decision? Have I considered that a whistleblower usually emerges and that secrets rarely stay secret? Is there any problem that could arise beyond the ten-year time horizon that I should take into account?*

Unethical activities often spring from arrangements that fail to protect the ethical position of the organization, so it is wise to pose some sniff tests about the organizational framework that spawns decisions, such as: *Do personnel in this area understand the organization's ethical expectations? Are personnel in a position where the gain from unethical activity can outweigh the chance of being found out or the penalty involved? Is there a timely ethics audit or review of activities and organizational arrangements in this area?*

Sniff tests can be helpful, even essential. David Nitkin, whose work at EthicScan created the concept, believes that sniff tests represent a means for top executives to have confidence that all their personnel can and will apply a consistent set of tests and, as a result, reach similar conclusions to ethical dilemmas. Wouldn't you rather head off an ethical dilemma that smells before it is too late?

LAW CASE SUMMARY: CAREMARK NATIONAL INC.

Reprinted with permission of the author, Prof. L.J. Brooks. All rights reserved.

Late in 1996, the Chancery Court of the State of Delaware, a very influential court in corporate matters, handed down a decision that changed the expectations of directors for monitoring the affairs of the organizations they direct. The change held in the *Caremark National Inc. Case* was to require directors to monitor organizational activities even when there is no cause for suspicion of wrongdoing.

Until the *Caremark* decision, the guiding case was the Delaware Supreme Court's 1963 decision in *Graham v. Allis-Chalmers Manufacturing Co. In Allis-Chalmers*, a case involving director's liability for violations of U.S. antitrust laws, the Court had found that, "absent cause for suspicion," a board of directors had no legal duty to create a system for monitoring or compliance of organizational activities. This allowed directors to argue an ostrich defence in the event of wrongdoing to the effect that they had, "seen no evil nor heard no evil," and had made their decisions in good faith and to the best of their ability. As a result, the fiduciary duties of directors, and the duty of care were somewhat circumscribed from the level of responsibility that some stakeholders felt reasonable.

The Chancery Court took the view in the *Caremark Case*, a derivative lawsuit involving kickbacks to health care providers in violation of the federal Anti-Referral Payments Law, that the directors could be liable for recovery of some of the company's $250 million in fines from its directors for breach of their duty of care by failing to take good faith measures to prevent or remedy the violations. The Court noted, since employee actions could prevent a corporation from achieving its strategic goals, "that a director's obligation includes a duty to assure in good faith that [an] information reporting system, which the Board concludes is adequate, exists and that failure to do so under some circumstances may, in theory at least, render a director liable for losses caused by non-compliance with applicable legal standards." Moreover, due to the issuance of the U.S. Federal Sentencing Guidelines on November 1, 1991, and their subsequent integration into expectations, directors must now consider the due diligence defence criteria that those guidelines have spawned when advancing their good faith defence. This means that the Chancery Court no longer considers a corporate compliance and monitoring program to be optional.

For further information, the reader is referred to an article by Frank M. Placenti in *The National Law Journal*, on Monday June 23, 1997 (pages B5, B6). Further insights are possible if higher courts modify the Chancery Court's *Caremark* decision. But until then, directors are well advised to be ethically proactive in the development of strategic plans, operating policies and in the monitoring of performance.

Jim Goodfellow and Allan Willis, "CEO Challenge," *CAmagazine* 40:1 (2007): 35–42.

Reproduced with permission from CAmagazine, published by the Canadian Institute of Chartered Accountants, Toronto.

In three short years, chief executive and chief financial officers have been required to certify financial info in the name of bolstering integrity

"Since 2004, three waves of CEO and CFO certification have washed over corporate Canada, and there are more to come. All are aimed at restoring investor confidence in financial reporting and related controls by improving accountability and transparency – terms seldom heard during the '90s, a time of heady growth, but which, since 2001, have resurfaced as key business, governance and disclosure principles.

Certification was introduced to Canada in 2004 when the Canadian Securities Administrators (CSA) required the CEO and CFO of a reporting issuer to certify the financial information in quarterly and annual filings. In 2005, that was expanded to include certification about disclosure controls and procedures. Last year, the third wave arrived. It requires certifying officers of TSX and TSX-V issuers to file the full annual certificate for financial years ending on or after June 30, 2006 – which, for many reporting issuers, means the calendar year ended December 31, 2006.

The full annual certificate in CSA Multilateral Instrument 52-109 expands the certification to require CEOs and CFOs to state they have "designed such internal control over financial reporting, or caused it to be designed under our supervision, to provide reasonable assurance regarding the reliability of financial reporting and the preparation of financial statements for external purposes in accordance with the issuer's GAAP."

In addition, they are required to certify that the annual Management's Discussion and Analysis (MD&A) discloses any changes in internal control over financial reporting (ICFR) that occurred in the latest interim reporting period that have materially affected, or could materially affect, the ICFR.

This third wave of certification applies only to the design of ICFR, not its operating effectiveness. That will be introduced in a fourth wave of certification, yet to come.

In March 2006, CSA Notice 52-313 announced that the CEO and CFO certificates of TSX and TSX-V issuers will be expanded to include certification of the effectiveness of the issuer's ICFR as of the end of the financial year and certification that the certifiers have "caused the issuer to disclose in the annual MD&A [their] conclusions about the effectiveness of internal control over financial reporting." The CSA's proposed rules for this fourth wave of certification were to be released by the end of 2006. (At press time they had yet to be published.)

As the certifications for Canadian reporting issuers continue to unfold, they will take a direction different from certification rules in the US. Unlike Securities Exchange Commission registrants, issuers in Canada will not, according to CSA Notice 52-313, be required to provide a separate management report on ICFR, nor will they have to obtain their auditor's opinion from an internal control audit or an opinion on man-agement's assessment of the effectiveness of ICFR.

Readers may wish to review the CSA's proposals in addition to the discussion here, which focuses on helping CEOs and CFOs, their management teams and their audit committees finalize the assessment of ICFR design and the disclosures needed in their annual MD&A to meet the certification requirements from June 2006 onward.

The top-down, risk-based approach

The current requirement to assess the design of ICFR creates a challenge. In effect, it requires certifying that ICFR exists on paper, without requiring testing as to whether it actually works in practice, especially during any particular reporting period. Therefore CEOs and CFOs need an organized, disciplined and documented process for assessing and documenting their conclusions concerning the design of ICFR in order to support their certification and MD&A disclosures.

The September 2006 CICA publication Internal Control 2006: The Next Wave of Certification provides a straightforward, business-focused, top-down and risk-based approach for CEOs and CFOs to follow in assessing and certifying the design of ICFR. This approach will also help companies prepare for the future evaluation of the effectiveness of ICFR.

To be effective and efficient, a top-down, risk-based approach requires at least two things. First, there must be a focus on the tone at the top, that is, the interaction between the board of directors and the CEO in establishing the control environment and the culture of integrity. Second, there must be a sound process for identifying principal business risks, including financial reporting and disclosure risks. The effectiveness of a top-down, risk-based approach to assessing ICFR design is consistent with findings reported in the August 2006 paper Internal Controls – A Review of Recent Developments issued by the International Federation of Accountants. This notes a convergence of thinking over the past two years in various countries' and bodies' pronouncements about internal control, emphasizing the importance of the tone at the top and a focus on risk as the essential features of internal control.

Further, companies should view their assessment of ICFR as a business improvement opportunity, not just a regulatory com-pliance task. The assessment of ICFR presents management, boards of directors and audit committees with the opportunity to reassess what ICFR is intended to achieve: control over financial reporting and disclosure risks. Companies should design and implement ICFR to achieve their business objectives as well as satisfying their external reporting obligations. After all, without effective ICFR, how can senior management and boards of directors be certain that decisions taken on the basis of internal financial information are being made on a sound basis?

The International Federation of Accountants paper stated an interesting finding from a recent UK review of its internal control code: "It was felt that those companies that viewed internal control as sound business practice were more likely to have embedded it into their normal business processes, and more likely to feel that they had benefited as a result, than those that viewed it primarily as a compliance exercise."

In summary, the tone at the top and the control environment, a focus on risk, the extent of active CEO involvement and appropriate board oversight are critical elements of ICFR. A top-down, risk-based approach is also likely to be more practical than the approach taken to date in the US for satisfying Section 404 of the Sarbanes-Oxley Act.

Accountability and transparency

The CSA's certification regulations are basedon two fundamental principles: accountability and transparency. The accountability principle is achieved through separate and personal certifications from the CEO and the CFO.

The transparency principle is applied at four levels. The first, the content level, refers to the degree to which the information in the filings enables readers to reliably assess and interpret the financial condition, results of operations and cash flows of the issuer. The second level, a process level, refers to the reliability of disclosure controls and procedures (DC&P), and disclosures of any material weakness in them. Now, the third level – also of process – has been added to address the design of ICFR and include disclosures about changes in ICFR. In future, as a fourth level, there will have to

be disclosures arising from management's conclusions from their evaluation of the effectiveness of ICFR.

Unfortunately, many issuers seem to have missed the messages about
transparency and accountability, which are embedded in the CSA disclosure requirements. The certification requirements about DC&P call for
CEOs and CFOs to state that they have caused the issuer to disclose in the
annual MD&A their conclusions about the effectiveness of the DC&P as of
the end of the period covered by the annual filings.

However, based on a sample of 286 issuers selected from across the
country, the CSA found, according to CSA Staff Notice 52-315 in September
2006, that: "Approximately 28% of issuers in our sample, however, failed to
include this disclosure in their annual MD&A. This widespread noncom-
pliance with such a clear and basic requirement shows that many issuers
are not paying adequate attention to their disclosure obligations. We are
particularly concerned by the failure to include the disclosure regarding
disclosure controls and procedures in the annual MD&A given that, in
most cases, the certifying officers specifically represented in their certificates that they had caused the issuer to include this disclosure in the
annual MD&A."

Clearly, this disclosure requirement has hit the CSA's radar screen, and it
will undoubtedly continue monitoring compliance with it.

What is less clear is whether the CSA will expand its focus to assess the
level of effort CEOs and CFOs are putting into their assessment of DC&P, or
to assess whether any material weaknesses exist in it. Perhaps it will take
challenges and decisions in the courts under civil liability to ultimately clarify the expectations and consequences concerning the judgments made in
the process of the evaluations and related personal certifications.

Materiality

Materiality in relation to a design weakness should be based on the extent
to which it would increase the risk that errors that could mislead investors
would be made or not be detected in the issuer's published financial statements prepared in accordance with the issuer's GAAP.

The accounting literature contains guidance in making materiality deter-
minations from both qualitative and quantitative perspectives. Unfortunately, little Canadian guidance is available to help management evaluate
the likelihood of errors occurring, or what would constitute a low versus
high likelihood. Current US guidance – Rule 2 of the US Public Company
Accounting Oversight Board – defines a material weakness as "a significant control deficiency, or combination of deficiencies, that results in a
more than remote likelihood that a material misstatement of the annual or

interim financial statements will not be prevented or detected." The bottom line is CEOs and CFOs must use their professional judgment in assessing their findings with respect to the design of ICFR and determining the appropriate disclosure in the MD&A.

Three levels of disclosure may be considered in evaluating a weakness in the design of ICFR:

- Type A – weaknesses considered material, which should be disclosed in the MD&A as well as to the audit committee and external auditors
- Type B – weaknesses not considered material but significant enough to be communicated to the audit committee and external auditors, and
- Type C – weaknesses that are not significant from an external reporting perspective but should be communicated to the appropriate member of management for remediation.

CEOs and CFOs should develop, in consultation with internal auditors, external auditors and the audit committee, their own criteria for applying these categories in practice.

Disclosure in the MD&A

The CSA Staff Notice 52-316 in September 2006 has made it clear that the CEO's and CFO's individual conclusions about the effectiveness of the DC&P should include the disclosure of identified weaknesses in ICFR:

> "Given the substantial overlap between the definitions of DC&P and ICFR, it is our view that the certifying officers therefore should cause the issuer to disclose in the annual MD&A the nature of any weakness [this is taken to mean any weakness that would cause the certifying officers to doubt whether the design of ICFR provides reasonable assurance regarding the reliability of the financial statements and whether they are in accordance with the issuer's GAAP] in the design of the issuer's ICFR, the risks associated with the weakness and the issuer's plan, if any, to remediate the weakness. If no such plan exists, theissuer should consider disclosing its reasons for not planning to remediate the weakness."

As a matter of prudence, management should also investigate and correct any financial statement errors that may have occurred as a result of the ICFR design weakness in the current reporting period and in future reporting periods until the weakness is remediated.

Deciding disclosure

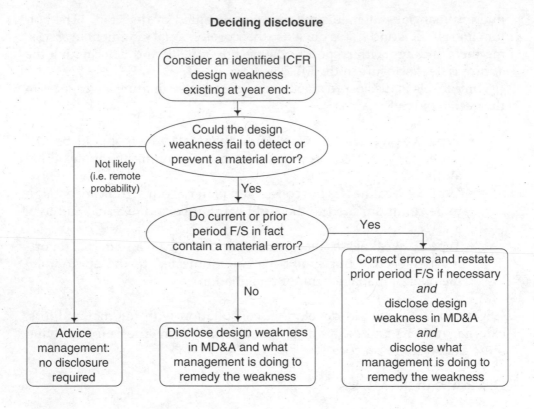

For example, suppose a material weakness in the design of ICFR is detected and disclosed in the 2006 annual MD&A. Management should conduct an investigation to ensure this weakness did not result in material errors in the 2006 financial statements before these statements are finalized and released. Then they should conduct a similar investigation in the first quarter of 2007, and in subsequent quarters, until the ICFR design weakness is corrected. To do otherwise could leave the CEO, CFO and the company's directors exposed to legal and/or regulatory actions if there were a material error in the financial statements and they had done nothing to ensure the financial statements were fairly presented when they were aware that a material design weakness existed in ICFR.

The chart "Deciding disclosure," may be helpful to CEOs and CFOs in deciding about MD&A disclosures of weaknesses in ICFR design.

The CEO/CFO certificate for 2006 also requires CEOs and CFOs to disclose in the MD&A any material changes in their ICFR that were made in the most recent interim reporting period (e.g., fourth quarter for annual MD&As). This applies to changesthat have materially affected ICFR and those that are reasonably likely to do so in the future.

Q4 change disclosure

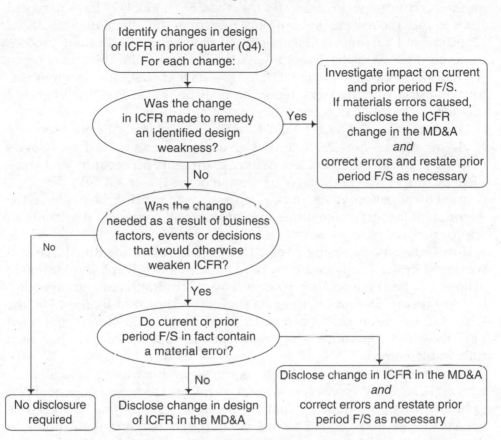

The chart "Q4 change disclosure," page 38, may be helpful in deciding about disclosures of fourth-quarter changes in ICFR design.

Signing certificates when material ICFR weaknesses exist

CEOs and CFOs will face a dilemma when they come to sign their certificates in situations where:

- an uncorrected material weakness in the design of ICFR has been identified as of the end of the reporting period,
- appropriate MD&A disclosure has been made about the weakness, and
- appropriate steps have been taken to ensure the weakness has had no material effect on the financial statements.

The wording of the required certification cannot be altered or amended and the certificate explicitly states that the CEO and CFO "have designed ICFR to provide reasonable assurance regarding the reliability of financial reporting and the preparation of financial statements for external purposes in accordance with the issuer's GAAP." However, the disclosure of an ICFR design weakness in the MD&A suggests that reasonable assurance as to the reliability of financial reporting does not exist. Faced with such a dilemma, what are CEOs and CFOs to do?

The September 2006 CSA Staff Notice 52-316 stated, "In our view, the certifying officers can certify the design of the issuer's ICFR if the issuer's disclosure about the identified weakness presents an accurate and complete picture of the condition of the design of the issuer's ICFR."

In such a situation, CEOs and CFOs are advised to bring the matter to the attention of the audit committee and consult legal counsel to determine an appropriate course of action.

If the issuer is disclosing a remediation plan for an identified material weakness in ICFR, it would be wise for that plan to clearly indicate what actions will be taken and when, as well as the commitment and capability to carry them out. Further, the plan should be approved by the CFO, the CEO and the audit committee and the disclosures should be continued until the audit committee is satisfied that the remediation plan has been fully implemented.

Management and audit committees are advised not to try to rationalize why an ICFR design weakness is not material and therefore does not need to be disclosed, in order to avoid the contradiction that might otherwise appear to arise between the disclosures in the MD&A and the wording in the required certificates.

Implications for smaller issuers

Small companies with limited resources may have certain ICFR design weaknesses (e.g., segregation of duties) that are difficult or wholly unreasonable to rectify. Because of this, many small companies may need to conclude that their ICFR is ineffective. They will, therefore, have to disclose the material weaknesses in ICFR in the MD&A and also, by consequence, have to report in the MD&A that their disclosure controls are ineffective.

As noted above, the CSA's Staff Notice 52-316 indicated in September 2006 that issuers should "disclose in the annual MD&A the nature of any weakness in the design of the issuer's ICFR, the risks associated with the weakness and the issuer's plan, if any, to remediate the weakness. If no such plan exists, the issuer should consider disclosing the reasons for not planning to remediate the weakness."

There are, however, actions that management and the audit committee may wish to consider that are less costly than re-mediating the ICFR design weakness, in order to provide investors with assurance that the ICFR design weaknesses have not resulted in material error in the financial statements. For example, the audit committee could engage the external auditor to perform quarterly reviews of interim financial statements. If the audit committee engages auditors to perform quarterly reviews, this fact should be disclosed in the MD&A.

Conclusion

The requirement to certify the design of ICFR cannot be avoided. Management can, however, carry out its ICFR design assessment process in a way that ensures ICFR supports both internal business decision-making and the reliability of external financial reporting. By taking such an approach, the time and effort spent in ICFR design and a top-down, risk-based assessment will be more likely to earn a return on the investment made. It may also help to support a due diligence defence by management and the board, should one ever be required. Finally, the actions taken and lessons learned now in assessing the design of ICFR will be of value in future when CEOs and CFOs face the fourth wave of certification – the annual evaluation of ICFR operating effectiveness.

Jim Goodfellow, FCA, is chair of the CICA's Canadian Performance Reporting Initiative-Board and partner at Deloitte & Touche LLP

Alan Willis, CA, is an independent consultant in corporate governance, performance measurement and performance reporting. He coauthored with Jim Goodfellow CICA's September 2006 guidance for management and directors, Internal Control 2006: The Next Wave of Certification

Lynn Sharp Paine, "Managing for Organizational Integrity," *Harvard Business Review* **March–April (1994): 106–117.**

Many managers think of ethics as a question of personal scruples, a confidential matter between individuals and their consciences. These executives are quick to describe any wrongdoing as an isolated incident, the work of a rogue employee. The thought that the company could bear any responsibility for an individual's misdeeds never enters their minds. Ethics, after all, has nothing to do with management.

In fact, ethics has *everything* to do with management. Rarely do the character flaws of a lone actor fully explain corporate misconduct. More typically, unethical business practice involves the tacit, if not explicit, cooperation of others and reflects the values, attitudes, beliefs, language, and behavioral patterns that define an organization's operating culture. Ethics, then, is as much an organizational as a personal issue. Managers who fail to provide proper leadership and to institute systems that facilitate ethical conduct share responsibility with those who conceive, execute, and knowingly benefit from corporate misdeeds.

Managers must acknowledge their role in shaping organizational ethics and seize this opportunity to create a climate that can strengthen the relationships and reputations on which their companies' success depends. Executives who ignore ethics run the risk of personal and corporate liability in today's increasingly tough legal environment. In addition, they deprive their organizations of the benefits available under new federal guidelines for sentencing organizations convicted of wrongdoing. These sentencing guidelines recognize for the first time the organizational and managerial roots of unlawful conduct and base fines partly on the extent to which companies have taken steps to prevent that misconduct.

Prompted by the prospect of leniency, many companies are rushing to implement compliance-based ethics programs. Designed by corporate counsel, the goal of these programs is to prevent, detect, and punish legal violations. But organizational ethics means more than avoiding illegal practice; and providing employees with a rule book will do little to address the problems underlying unlawful conduct. To foster a climate that encourages exemplary behavior, corporations need a comprehensive approach that goes beyond the often punitive legal compliance stance.

An integrity-based approach to ethics management combines a concern for the law with an emphasis on managerial responsibility for ethical behavior. Though integrity strategies may vary in design and scope, all strive to define companies' guiding values, aspirations, and patterns of thought and conduct. When integrated into the day-to-day operations of an organization, such strategies can help prevent damaging ethical lapses while tapping into powerful human impulses for moral thought and action. Then an ethical framework becomes no longer a burdensome constraint within which companies must operate, but the governing ethos of an organization.

How Organizations Shape Individuals' Behavior

The once familiar picture of ethics as individualistic, unchanging, and impervious to organizational influences has not stood up to scrutiny in recent years. Sears Auto Centers' and Beech-Nut Nutrition Corporation's experiences illustrate the role organizations play in shaping individuals' behavior – and how even sound moral fiber can fray when stretched too thin.

In 1992, Sears, Roebuck & Company was inundated with complaints about its automotive service business. Consumers and attorneys general in more than 40 states had accused the company of misleading customers and selling them unnecessary parts and services, from brake jobs to front-end alignments. It would be a mistake, however, to see this situation exclusively in terms of any one individual's moral failings. Nor did management set out to defraud Sears customers. Instead, a number of organizational factors contributed to the problematic sales practices.

In the face of declining revenues, shrinking market share, and an increasingly competitive market for undercar services, Sears management attempted to spur the performance of its auto centers by introducing new goals and incentives for employees. The company increased minimum work quotas and introduced productivity incentives for mechanics. The automotive service advisers were given product-specific sales quotas – sell so many springs, shock absorbers, alignments, or brake jobs per shift – and paid a commission based on sales. According to advisers, failure to meet quotas could lead to a transfer or a reduction in work hours. Some employees spoke of the "pressure, pressure, pressure" to bring in sales.

Under this new set of organizational pressures and incentives, with few options for meeting their sales goals legitimately, some employees' judgment understandably suffered. Management's failure to clarify the line between unnecessary service and legitimate preventive maintenance, coupled with consumer ignorance, left employees to chart their own courses through a vast gray area, subject to a wide range of interpretations. Without active management support for ethical practice and mechanisms to detect and check questionable sales methods and poor work, it is not surprising that some employees may have reacted to contextual forces by resorting to exaggeration, carelessness, or even misrepresentation.

Shortly after the allegations against Sears became public, CEO Edward Brennan acknowledged management's responsibility for putting in place compensation and goal-setting systems that "created an environment in which mistakes did occur." Although the company denied any intent to deceive consumers, senior executives eliminated commissions for service advisers and discontinued sales quotas for specific parts. They also instituted a system of unannounced shopping audits and made plans to expand the internal monitoring of service. In settling the pending lawsuits, Sears offered coupons to customers who had bought certain auto services between 1990 and 1992. The total cost of the settlement, including potential customer refunds, was an estimated $60 million.

Contextual forces can also influence the behavior of top management, as a former CEO of Beech-Nut Nutrition Corporation discovered. In the early 1980s, only two years after joining the company, the CEO found evidence suggesting that the apple juice concentrate, supplied by the company's vendors for use in Beech-Nut's "100% pure" apple juice, contained nothing more than sugar water and chemicals. The CEO could have destroyed the bogus inventory and withdrawn the juice from grocers' shelves, but he was under extraordinary pressure to turn the ailing company around. Eliminating the inventory would have killed any hope of turning even the meager $700,000 profit promised to Beech-Nut's then parent, Nestlé.

A number of people in the corporation, it turned out, had doubted the purity of the juice for several years before the CEO arrived. But the 25 percent price advantage offered by the supplier of the bogus concentrate allowed the operations head to meet cost-control goals. Furthermore, the company lacked an effective quality control system, and a conclusive lab test for juice purity did not yet exist. When a member of the research department voiced concerns about the juice to operating management, he was accused of not being a team player and of acting like "Chicken Little." His judgment, his supervisor wrote in an annual performance review, was "colored by naiveté and impractical ideals." No one else seemed to have considered the company's obligations to its customers or to have thought about the potential harm of disclosure. No one considered the fact that the sale of adulterated or misbranded juice is a legal offense, putting the company and its top management at risk of criminal liability.

An FDA investigation taught Beech-Nut the hard way. In 1987, the company pleaded guilty to selling adulterated and misbranded juice. Two years and two criminal trials later, the CEO pleaded guilty to ten counts of mislabeling. The total cost to the company – including fines, legal expenses, and lost sales – was an estimated $25 million.

Such errors of judgment rarely reflect an organizational culture and management philosophy that sets out to harm or deceive. More often, they reveal a culture that is insensitive or indifferent to ethical considerations or one that lacks effective organizational systems. By the same token, exemplary conduct usually reflects an organizational culture and philosophy that is infused with a sense of responsibility.

For example, Johnson & Johnson's handling of the Tylenol crisis is sometimes attributed to the singular personality of then-CEO James Burke. However, the decision to do a nationwide recall of Tylenol capsules in order to avoid further loss of life from product tampering was in reality not one decision but thousands of decisions made by individuals at all levels of the organization. The "Tylenol decision," then, is best understood not as an isolated incident, the achievement of a lone individual, but as the reflection of an organization's culture. Without a shared set of values and guiding principles deeply ingrained throughout the organization, it is doubtful that Johnson & Johnson's response would have been as rapid, cohesive, and ethically sound.

Many people resist acknowledging the influence of organizational factors on individual behavior – especially on misconduct – for fear of diluting people's sense of personal moral responsibility. But this fear is based on a false dichotomy between holding individual transgressors accountable and holding "the system" accountable. Acknowledging the importance of organizational context need not imply exculpating individual wrongdoers. To understand all is not to forgive all.

The Limits of a Legal Compliance Program

The consequences of an ethical lapse can be serious and far-reaching. Organizations can quickly become entangled in an all-consuming web of legal proceedings. The risk of litigation and liability has increased in the past decade as lawmakers have legislated new civil and criminal offenses, stepped up penalties, and improved support for law enforcement. Equally – if not more – important is the damage an ethical lapse can do to an organization's reputation and relationships. Both Sears and Beech-Nut, for instance, struggled to regain consumer trust and market share long after legal proceedings had ended.

Corporate Fines Under the Federal Sentencing Guidelines

What size fine is a corporation likely to pay if convicted of a crime? It depends on a number of factors, some of which are beyond a CEO's control, such as the existence of a prior record of similar misconduct. But it also depends on more controllable factors. The most important of these are reporting and accepting responsibility for the crime, cooperating with authorities, and having an effective program in place to prevent and detect unlawful behavior.

The following example, based on a case studied by the United States Sentencing Commission, shows how the *1991 Federal Sentencing Guidelines* have affected overall fine levels and how managers' actions influence organizational fines.

Acme Corporation was charged and convicted of mail fraud. The company systematically charged customers who damaged rented automobiles more than the actual cost of repairs. Acme also billed some customers for the cost of repairs to vehicles for which they were not responsible. Prior to the criminal adjudication, Acme paid $13.7 million in restitution to the customers who had been overcharged.

Deciding before the enactment of the sentencing guidelines, the judge in the criminal case imposed a fine of $6.85 million, roughly half the pecuniary loss suffered by Acme's customers. Under the sentencing guidelines, however, the results could have been dramatically different. Acme could have been fined anywhere from 5 percent to 200 percent the loss suffered by customers, depending on whether or not it had an effective program to prevent and detect violations of law and on whether or not it reported the crime, cooperated with authorities, and accepted responsibility for the unlawful conduct. If a high ranking official at Acme were found to have been involved, the maximum fine could have been as large as $54,800,000 or four times the loss to Acme customers. The following chart shows a possible range of fines for each situation:

WHAT FINE CAN ACME EXPECT?

	Maximum	Minimum
Program, reporting, cooperation, responsibility	$ 2,740,000	$ 685,000
Program only	10,960,000	5,480,000
No program, no reporting no cooperation, no responsibility	27,400,000	13,700,000
No program, no reporting no cooperation, no responsibility, involvement of high-level personnel	54,800,000	27,400,000

Based on *Case No.: 88-266, United States Sentencing Commission, Supplementary Report on Sentencing Guidelines for Organizations.*

As more managers have become alerted to the importance of organizational ethics, many have asked their lawyers to develop corporate ethics programs to detect and prevent violations of the law. The *1991 Federal Sentencing Guidelines* offer a compelling rationale. Sanctions such as fines and probation for organizations convicted of wrongdoing can vary dramatically depending both on the degree of management cooperation in reporting and investigating corporate misdeeds and on whether or not the company has implemented a legal compliance program. (See the insert "Corporate Fines Under the Federal Sentencing Guidelines.")

Such programs tend to emphasize the prevention of unlawful conduct, primarily by increasing surveillance and control and by imposing penalties for wrongdoers. While plans vary, the basic framework is outlined in the sentencing guidelines. Managers must establish compliance standards and procedures; designate high-level personnel to oversee compliance; avoid delegating discretionary authority to those likely to act unlawfully; effectively communicate the company's standards and procedures through training or publications; take reasonable steps to achieve compliance through audits, monitoring processes, and a system for employees to report criminal misconduct without fear of retribution; consistently enforce standards through appropriate disciplinary measures; respond appropriately when offenses are detected; and, finally, take reasonable steps to prevent the occurrence of similar offenses in the future.

There is no question of the necessity of a sound, well-articulated strategy for legal compliance in an organization. After all, employees can be frustrated and frightened by the complexity of today's legal environment. And even managers who claim to use the law as a guide to ethical behavior often lack more than a rudimentary understanding of complex legal issues.

Managers would be mistaken, however, to regard legal compliance as an adequate means for addressing the full range of ethical issues that arise every day. "If it's legal, it's ethical," is a frequently heard slogan; but conduct that is lawful may be highly problematic from an ethical point of view. Consider the sale in some countries of hazardous products without appropriate warnings or the purchase of goods from suppliers who operate inhumane sweatshops in developing countries. Companies engaged in international business often discover that conduct that infringes on recognized standards of human rights and decency is legally permissible in some jurisdictions.

Legal clearance does not certify the absence of ethical problems in the United States either, as a 1991 case at Salomon Brothers illustrates. Four top-level executives failed to take appropriate action when learning of unlawful activities on the government trading desk. Company lawyers found no law obligating the executives to disclose the improprieties. Nevertheless, the executives' delay in disclosing and failure to reveal their prior knowledge prompted a serious crisis of confidence among employees, creditors, shareholders, and customers.

The executives were forced to resign, having lost the moral authority to lead. Their ethical lapse compounded the trading desk's legal offenses, and the company ended up suffering losses – including legal costs, increased funding costs, and lost business – estimated at nearly $1 billion.

A compliance approach to ethics also overemphasizes the threat of detection and punishment in order to channel behavior in lawful directions. The underlying model for this approach is deterrence theory, which envisions people as rational maximizers of self-interest, responsive to the personal costs and benefits of their choices, yet indifferent to the moral legitimacy of those choices. But a recent study reported in *Why People Obey the Law* by Tom R. Tyler shows that obedience to the law is strongly influenced by a belief in its legitimacy and its moral correctness. People generally feel that they have a strong obligation to obey the law. Education about the legal standards and a supportive environment may be all that's required to insure compliance.

Discipline is, of course, a necessary part of any ethical system. Justified penalties for the infringement of legitimate norms are fair and appropriate. Some people do need the threat of sanctions. However, an overemphasis on potential sanctions can be superfluous and even counterproductive. Employees may rebel against programs that stress penalties, particularly if they are designed and imposed without employee involvement or if the standards are vague or unrealistic. Management may talk of mutual trust when unveiling a compliance plan, but employees often see a warning from on high. Indeed, the more skeptical among them may view compliance programs as nothing more than liability insurance for senior management. This is not an unreasonable conclusion, considering that compliance programs rarely address the root causes of misconduct.

Even in the best cases, legal compliance is unlikely to unleash much moral imagination or commitment. The law does not generally seek to inspire human excellence or distinction. It is no guide for exemplary behavior – or even good practice. Those managers who define ethics as legal compliance are implicitly endorsing a code of moral mediocrity for their organizations. As Richard Breeden, former chairman of the Securities and Exchange Commission, noted, "It is not an adequate ethical standard to aspire to get through the day without being indicted."

Integrity as a Governing Ethic

A strategy based on integrity holds organizations to a more robust standard. While compliance is rooted in avoiding legal sanctions, organizational integrity is based on the concept of self-governance in accordance with a set of guiding principles. From the perspective of integrity, the task of ethics management is to define and give life to an organization's guiding values, to create an environment that supports ethically sound behavior, and to instill a sense of shared accountability among employees. The need to obey the law is viewed as a positive aspect of organizational life, rather than an unwelcome constraint imposed by external authorities.

An integrity strategy is characterized by a conception of ethics as a driving force of an enterprise. Ethical values shape the search for opportunities, the design of organizational systems, and the decision-making process used by individuals and groups. They provide a common frame of reference and serve as a unifying force across different functions, lines of business, and employee groups. Organizational ethics helps define what a company is and what it stands for.

Many integrity initiatives have structural features common to compliance-based initiatives: a code of conduct, training in relevant areas of law, mechanisms for reporting and investigating potential misconduct, and audits and controls to insure that laws and company standards are being met. In addition, if suitably designed, an integrity-based initiative can establish a foundation for seeking the legal benefits that are available under the sentencing guidelines should criminal wrongdoing occur. (See the insert, "The Hallmarks of an Effective Integrity Strategy.")

But an integrity strategy is broader, deeper, and more demanding than a legal compliance initiative. Broader in that it seeks to enable responsible conduct. Deeper in that it cuts to the ethos and operating systems of the organization and its members, their guiding values and patterns of thought and action. And more demanding in that it requires an active effort to define the responsibilities and aspirations that constitute an organization's ethical compass. Above all, organizational ethics is seen as the work of management. Corporate counsel may play a role in the design and implementation of integrity strategies, but managers at all levels and across all functions are involved in the process. (See the chart, "Strategies for Ethics Management.")

During the past decade, a number of companies have undertaken integrity initiatives. They vary according to the ethical values focused on and the implementation approaches used. Some companies focus on the core values of integrity that reflect basic social obligations, such as respect for the rights of others, honesty, fair dealing, and obedience to the law. Other companies emphasize aspirations – values that are ethically desirable but not necessarily morally obligatory – such as good service to customers, a commitment to diversity, and involvement in the community.

When it comes to implementation, some companies begin with behavior. Following Aristotle's view that one becomes courageous by acting as a courageous person, such companies develop codes of conduct specifying appropriate behavior, along with a system of incentives, audits, and controls. Other companies focus less on specific actions and more on developing attitudes, decision-making processes, and ways of thinking that reflect their values. The assumption is that personal commitment and appropriate decision processes will lead to right action.

Martin Marietta, NovaCare, and Wetherill Associates have implemented and lived with quite different integrity strategies. In each case, management has found that the initiative has made important and often unexpected contributions to competitiveness, work environment, and key relationships on which the company depends.

Martin Marietta: Emphasizing Core Values

Martin Marietta Corporation, the U.S. aerospace and defense contractor, opted for an integrity-based ethics program in 1985. At the time, the defense industry was under attack for fraud and mismanagement, and Martin Marietta was under investigation for improper travel billings. Managers knew they needed a better form of self-governance but were skeptical that an ethics program could influence behavior. "Back then people asked, 'Do you really need an ethics program to be ethical?'" recalls current President Thomas Young. "Ethics was something personal. Either you had it, or you didn't."

The corporate general counsel played a pivotal role in promoting the program, and legal compliance was a critical objective. But it was conceived of and implemented from the start as a company-wide management initiative aimed at creating and maintaining a "do-it-right" climate. In its original conception, the program emphasized core values, such as honesty and fair play. Over time, it expanded to encompass quality and environmental responsibility as well.

Today the initiative consists of a code of conduct, an ethics training program, and procedures for reporting and investigating ethical concerns within the company. It also includes a system for disclosing violations of federal procurement law to the government. A corporate ethics office manages the program, and ethics representatives are stationed at major facili-

The Hallmarks of an Effective Integrity Strategy

There is no one right integrity strategy. Factors such as management personality, company history, culture, lines of business, and industry regulations must be taken into account when shaping an appropriate set of values and designing an implementation program. Still, several features are common to efforts that have achieved some success:

☐ *The guiding values and commitments make sense and are clearly communicated.* They reflect important organizational obligations and widely shared aspirations that appeal to the organization's members. Employees at all levels take them seriously, feel comfortable discussing them, and have a concrete understanding of their practical importance. This does not signal the absence of ambiguity and conflict but a willingness to seek solutions compatible with the framework of values.

☐ *Company leaders are personally committed, credible, and willing to take action on the values they espouse.* They are not mere mouthpieces. They are willing to scrutinize their own decisions. Consistency on the part of leadership is key. Waffling on values will lead to employee cynicism and a rejection of the program. At the same time, managers must assume responsibility for making tough calls when ethical obligations conflict.

☐ *The espoused values are integrated into the normal channels of management decision making and are reflected in the organization's critical activities:* the development of plans, the setting of goals, the search for opportunities, the allocation of resources, the gathering and communication of information, the measurement of performance, and the promotion and advancement of personnel.

☐ *The company's systems and structures support and reinforce its values.* Information systems, for example, are designed to provide timely and accurate information. Reporting relationships are structured to build in checks and balances to promote objective judgment. Performance appraisal is sensitive to means as well as ends.

☐ *Managers throughout the company have the decision-making skills, knowledge, and competencies needed to make ethically sound decisions on a day-to-day basis.* Ethical thinking and awareness must be part of every managers' mental equipment. Ethics education is usually part of the process.

Success in creating a climate for responsible and ethically sound behavior requires continuing effort and a considerable investment of time and resources. A glossy code of conduct, a high-ranking ethics officer, a training program, an annual ethics audit – these trappings of an ethics program do not necessarily add up to a responsible, law-abiding organization whose espoused values match its actions. A formal ethics program can serve as a catalyst and a support system, but organizational integrity depends on the integration of the company's values into its driving systems.

ties. An ethics steering committee, made up of Martin Marietta's president, senior executives, and two rotating members selected from field operations, oversees the ethics office. The audit and ethics committee of the board of directors oversees the steering committee.

The ethics office is responsible for responding to questions and concerns from the company's employees. Its network of representatives serves as a sounding board, a source of guidance, and a channel for raising a range of issues, from allegations of wrongdoing to complaints about poor management, unfair supervision, and company policies and practices. Martin Marietta's ethics network, which accepts anonymous complaints, logged over 9,000 calls in 1991, when the company had about 60,000 employees. In 1992, it investigated 684 cases. The ethics office also works closely with the human resources, legal, audit, communications, and security functions to respond to employee concerns.

Shortly after establishing the program, the company began its first round of ethics training for the entire workforce, starting with the CEO and senior executives. Now in its third round, training for senior executives focuses on decision making, the challenges of balancing multiple responsibilities, and compliance with laws and regulations critical to the company. The incentive compensation plan for executives makes responsibility for promoting ethical conduct an explicit requirement for reward eligibility and requires that business and personal goals be achieved in accordance with the company's policy on ethics. Ethical conduct and support for the ethics program are also criteria in regular performance reviews.

Today top-level managers say the ethics program has helped the company avoid serious problems and become more responsive to its more than 90,000 employees. The ethics network, which tracks the number and types of cases and complaints, has served as an early warning system for poor management, quality and safety defects, racial and gender discrimination, environmental concerns, inaccurate and false records, and personnel grievances regarding salaries, promotions, and layoffs. By providing an alternative channel for raising such concerns, Martin Marietta is able to take corrective action more quickly and with a lot less pain. In many cases, potentially embarrassing problems have been identified and dealt with before becoming a management crisis, a lawsuit, or a criminal investigation. Among employees who brought complaints in 1993, 75 percent were satisfied with the results.

Company executives are also convinced that the program has helped reduce the incidence of misconduct. When allegations of misconduct do surface, the company says it deals with them more openly. On several occasions, for instance, Martin Marietta has voluntarily disclosed and made restitution to the government for misconduct involving potential viola-tions of federal procurement laws. In addition, when an employee alleged that the company had retaliated against him for voicing safety concerns about his plant on CBS news, top management commissioned an investiga-tion by an outside law firm. Although failing to support the allegations, the investigation found that employees at the plant feared retaliation when raising health, safety, or environmental complaints. The company redou-bled its efforts to identify and discipline those employees taking retaliatory action and stressed the desirability of an open work environment in its eth-ics training and company communications.

Although the ethics program helps Martin Marietta avoid certain types of litigation, it has occasionally led to other kinds of legal action. In a few cases, employees dismissed for violating the code of ethics sued Martin Marietta, arguing that the company had violated its own code by imposing unfair and excessive discipline.

Still, the company believes that its attention to ethics has been worth it. The ethics program has led to better relationships with the government, as well as to new business opportunities. Along with prices and technology, Martin Marietta's record of integrity, quality, and reliability of estimates plays a role in the awarding of defense contracts, which account for some 75 percent of the company's revenues. Executives believe that the reputa-tion they've earned through their ethics program has helped them build trust with government auditors, as well. By opening up communications, the company has reduced the time spent on redundant audits.

The program has also helped change employees' perceptions and prior-ities. Some managers compare their new ways of thinking about ethics to the way they understand quality. They consider more carefully how situa-tions will be perceived by others, the possible long-term consequences of short-term thinking, and the need for continuous improvement. CEO Nor-man Augustine notes, "Ten years ago, people would have said that there were no ethical issues in business. Today employees think their number-one objective is to be thought of as decent people doing quality work."

NovaCare: Building Shared Aspirations

NovaCare Inc., one of the largest providers of rehabilitation services to nursing homes and hospitals in the United States, has oriented its ethics effort toward building a common core of shared aspirations. But in 1988, when the company was called InSpeech, the only sentiment shared was mutual mistrust.

Senior executives built the company from a series of aggressive acquisi-

```
+-------------------------------------------------------------------+
|                 STRATEGIES FOR ETHICS MANAGEMENT                  |
+-------------------------------------------------------------------+
```

Characteristics of Compliance Strategy		Characteristics of Integrity Strategy	
Ethos	Conformity with externally imposed standards	Ethos	Self-governance according to chosen standards
Objective	Prevent criminal misconduct	Objective	Enable responsible conduct
Leadership	Lawyer-driven	Leadership	Management-driven, with aid of lawyers, HR, others
Methods	Education, reduced discretion, auditing and controls, penalties	Methods	Education, leadership, accountability, organizational systems and decision processes, auditing and controls, penalties
Behavioral assumptions	Autonomous beings guided by material self-interest	Behavioral assumptions	Social beings guided by material self-interest, values, ideals, peers

Implementation of Compliance Strategy		Implementation of Integrity Strategy	
Standards	Criminal and regulatory law	Standards	Company values and aspirations; social obligations, including law
Staffing	Lawyers	Staffing	Executives and managers with lawyers, others
Activities	Develop compliance standards, train and communicate, handle reports of misconduct, conduct investigations, oversee compliance audits, enforce standards	Activities	Lead development of company values and standards, train and communicate, integrate into company systems, provide guidance and consultation, assess values performance, identify and resolve problems, oversee compliance activities
Education	Compliance standards and system	Education	Decision making and values compliance standards and system

tions over a brief period of time to take advantage of the expanding market for therapeutic services. However, in 1988, the viability of the company was in question. Turnover among its frontline employees – the clinicians and therapists who care for patients in nursing homes and hospitals – escalated to 57 per cent per year. The company's inability to retain therapists caused customers to defect and the stock price to languish in an extended slump.

After months of soul-searching, InSpeech executives realized that the turnover rate was a symptom of a more basic problem: the lack of a common set of values and aspirations. There was, as one executive put it, a "huge disconnect" between the values of the therapists and clinicians and those of the managers who ran the company. The therapists and clinicians evaluated the company's success in terms of its delivery of high-quality health care. In-Speech management, led by executives with financial services and venture capital backgrounds, measured the company's worth exclusively in terms of financial success. Management's single-minded emphasis on increasing hours of reimbursable care turned clinicians off. They took management's performance orientation for indifference to patient care and left the company in droves.

CEO John Foster recognized the need for a common frame of reference and a common language to unify the diverse groups. So he brought in consultants to conduct interviews and focus groups with the company's health care professionals, managers, and customers. Based on the results, an employee task force drafted a proposed vision statement for the company, and another 250 employees suggested revisions. Then Foster and several senior managers developed a succinct statement of the company's guiding purpose and fundamental beliefs that could be used as a framework for making decisions and setting goals, policies, and practices.

Unlike a code of conduct, which articulates specific behavioral standards, the statement of vision, purposes, and beliefs lays out in very simple terms the company's central purpose and core values. The purpose – meeting the rehabilitation needs of patients through clinical leadership – is supported by four key beliefs: respect for the individual, service to the customer, pursuit of excellence, and commitment to personal integrity. Each value is discussed with examples of how it is manifested in the day-to-day activities and policies of the company, such as how to measure the quality of care.

To support the newly defined values, the company changed its name to NovaCare and introduced a number of structural and operational changes. Field managers and clinicians were given greater decision-making authority; clinicians were provided with additional resources to assist in the delivery of effective therapy; and a new management structure integrated the various therapies offered by the company. The hiring of new corporate personnel with health care backgrounds reinforced the company's new clinical focus.

The introduction of the vision, purpose, and beliefs met with varied reactions from employees, ranging from cool skepticism to open enthusiasm. One employee remembered thinking the talk about values "much ado about nothing." Another recalled, "It was really wonderful. It gave us a goal that everyone aspired to, no matter what their place in the company." At first, some were baffled about how the vision, purpose, and beliefs were to be used. But, over time, managers became more adept at explaining and using them as a guide. When a customer tried to hire away a valued employee, for example, managers considered raiding the customer's company for employees. After reviewing the beliefs, the managers abandoned the idea.

NovaCare managers acknowledge and company surveys indicate that there is plenty of room for improvement. While the values are used as a firm reference point for decision making and evaluation in some areas of the company, they are still viewed with reservation in others. Some managers do not "walk the talk," employees complain. And recently acquired companies have yet to be fully integrated into the program. Nevertheless, many NovaCare employees say the values initiative played a critical role in the company's 1990 turnaround.

The values reorientation also helped the company deal with its most serious problem: turnover among health care providers. In 1990, the turnover rate stood at 32 percent, still above target but a significant improvement over the 1988 rate of 57 percent. By 1993, turnover had dropped to 27 percent. Moreover, recruiting new clinicians became easier. Barely able to hire 25 new clinicians each month in 1988, the company added 776 in 1990 and 2,546 in 1993. Indeed, one employee who left during the 1988 turmoil said that her decision to return in 1990 hinged on the company's adoption of the vision, purpose, and beliefs.

Wetherill Associates: Defining Right Action

Wetherill Associates, Inc. – a small, privately held supplier of electrical parts to the automotive market – has neither a conventional code of conduct nor a statement of values. Instead, WAI has a *Quality Assurance Manual* – a combination of philosophy text, conduct guide, technical manual, and company profile – that describes the company's commitment to honesty and its guiding principle of right action.

WAI doesn't have a corporate ethics officer who reports to top management, because at WAI, the company's corporate ethics officer *is* top management. Marie Bothe, WAI's chief executive officer, sees her main function as keeping the 350-employee company on the path of right action and looking for opportunities to help the community. She delegates the "technical" aspects of the business – marketing, finance, personnel, operations – to other members of the organization.

Right action, the basis for all of WAI's decisions, is a well-developed approach that challenges most conventional management thinking. The company explicitly rejects the usual conceptual boundaries that separate morality and self-interest. Instead, they define right behavior as logically, expediently, and morally right. Managers teach employees to look at the needs of the customers, suppliers, and the community – in addition to those of the company and its employees – when making decisions.

WAI also has a unique approach to competition. One employee explains, "We are not 'in competition' with anybody. We just do what we have to do to serve the customer." Indeed, when occasionally unable to fill orders, WAI salespeople refer customers to competitors. Artificial incentives, such as sales contests, are never used to spur individual performance. Nor are sales results used in determining compensation. Instead, the focus is on team-work and customer service. Managers tell all new recruits that absolute honesty, mutual courtesy, and respect are standard operating procedure.

Newcomers generally react positively to company philosophy, but not all are prepared for such a radical departure from the practices they have known elsewhere. Recalling her initial interview, one recruit described her response to being told that lying was not allowed, "What do you mean? No lying? I'm a buyer. I lie for a living!" Today she is persuaded that the policy makes sound business sense. WAI is known for informing suppliers of overshipments as well as undershipments and for scrupu-lous honesty in the sale of parts, even when deception cannot be readily detected.

Since its entry into the distribution business 13 years ago, WAI has seen its revenues climb steadily from just under $1 million to nearly $98 million in 1993, and this in an industry with little growth. Once seen as an upstart beset by naysayers and industry skeptics, WAI is now credited with enter-ing and professionalizing an industry in which kickbacks, bribes, and "gra-tuities" were commonplace. Employees – equal numbers of men and women ranging in age from 17 to 92 – praise the work environment as both productive and supportive.

WAI's approach could be difficult to introduce in a larger, more tradi-tional organization. WAI is a small company founded by 34 people who shared a belief in right action; its ethical values were naturally built into the organization from the start. Those values are so deeply ingrained in the company's culture and operating systems that they have been largely self-sustaining. Still, the company has developed its own training program and takes special care to hire people willing to support right action. Ethics and job skills are considered equally important in determining an individual's competence and suitability for employment. For WAI, the challenge will be to sustain its vision as the company grows and taps into markets overseas.

At WAI, as at Martin Marietta and NovaCare, a management-led commitment to ethical values has contributed to competitiveness, positive workforce morale, as well as solid sustainable relationships with the company's key constituencies. In the end, creating a climate that encourages exemplary conduct may be the best way to discourage damaging misconduct. Only in such an environment do rogues really act alone.

Source: Lynn Sharp Paine is a John G. McLean professor at the Harvard Business School, specializing in management ethics. Her current research focuses on leadership and organizational integrity in a global environment.

S. Prakash Sethi, "Codes of Conduct for Global Business: Prospects and Challenges of Implementation," *Principles of Stakeholder Management* **(Toronto: The Clarkson Centre for Business Ethics & Board Effectiveness, 1999), 9–20.**

Reprinted with permission of the Clarkson Centre for Business Ethics & Board Effectiveness, Rotman School of Management, Toronto. All rights reserved.

Corporate Codes and Critics

In the United States and Western Europe, corporate codes of conduct have become *de rigueur* for most large corporations. According to recent studies, 60 to 70 percent of major US corporations have issued codes of conduct, and many of the largest foreign multinationals have done so as well. These codes usually attempt to state the company's mission, values, and goals, and to describe its relationship to various stakeholders, both internal and external. Unfortunately, most of these codes suffer from a number of flaws:

- They are presented as public statements of lofty intent and purpose, but lack specific content.
- While they mention the corporation's commitment to its customers, employees, etc., they ignore the rights of these key stakeholders in their dealings with the company.
- They make no provisions for internal implementation, and code compliance is not integrated into the organization's procedures and reward structure; hence, managers and employees are often uninformed about the codes and their content, and do not take them seriously.
- They provide no basis or framework for communication with external communities about the efforts and results (success or failure) of the corporation in achieving the codes' objectives.

The inevitable result of these defects is that corporate codes of conduct are often treated with disdain by knowledgeable and influential opinion leaders among various stakeholder groups, as well as by outside analysts and the public at large. To be sure, there are a handful of companies whose codes of conduct are taken more seriously by their constituencies. Notable examples are those of Motorola, Levi Strauss, Texas Instruments, Sara Lee, and Mattel. However, the very smallness of this group reinforces my point. And, with the exception of Mattel, none of these corporations has chosen to make public either the process by which it seeks compliance of its code within its own organization (particularly by its overseas subsidiaries and strategic partners), or the results of its compliance efforts. Nor have the corporations, with the exception of Mattel, subjected their codes or processes to independent outside verification.

The weakness of corporate commitment to code compliance is all too apparent. After thirty years of research and teaching in this field, I can point to only one major corporation that has asked external independent monitors to examine its code compliance and has made the results public. This example is Nestle, the Swiss-based multinational corporation and one of the world's largest manufacturers of food and related products. Nestle was confronted with worldwide public boycotts of its products, and demonstrations by advocates of the poor and developing countries for its alleged improper marketing and promotional activities in the sale of infant formula products in these countries. Although inherently safe, these products were too expensive and largely unnecessary in these settings. Poor and uninformed mothers in developing countries were pressured into buying these products through intense promotion. Eventually, the World Health Organization enacted an International Code of Marketing of Breast-Milk Substitutes (Infant Formula Code) which banned most advertising and promotion of such products. Nestle was strongly opposed to the development of this Code. Nevertheless, after the Code was enacted, Nestle announced its willingness to abide by the Code and arranged for independent verification and compliance monitoring. The outcome was highly salutory. Within a period of less than four years, Nestle's reputation was largely restored, and the boycott against the company's products was called off.

Since that time, only one US multinational corporation has voluntarily promulgated a global code of conduct that committed itself to independent monitoring by an external group of credible and experienced persons charged to make a public report of their findings. That company is Mattel, one of the world's largest producers of children's *toys* including Barbie, Hot Wheels and Fisher Price products. This experience, and my personal involvement in it, will be further discussed below.

Corporate Response to Criticism

There have, of course, been a few other notable positive responses by major corporations, both individually and collectively, to public criticism. The promulgation of the Sullivan Principles by US firms operating in South Africa is a significant example. For the most part, however, multinational corporations have responded to public pressures in two lesseffective ways:

- They claim to abide by all local laws and standards. They also declare that their practices are driven by competitive market forces, low worker productivity, and the extra cost of doing business in different countries. Furthermore, they claim, often with some justification, that wages and working conditions in their own plants are superior to other plants in these areas.
- They promulgate voluntary codes of conduct that appear to address the concerns of their critics. Unfortunately, these weak and haphazard efforts often reveal the *absence* of long-term strategies to deal with underlying issues, as well as inadequate programs of public communication. Very few companies have created codes of conduct or "best practice" by which they can actually guide and evaluate their overseas operations, or the conduct of their local partners and suppliers.

Companies are often seen as being dragged into action only when public pressure becomes too intense to ignore. Alternatively, companies have resisted change by spending incredible amounts of time and effort in discussions about code formulation. This can be seen in the case of the apparel industry's code of conduct. President Clinton announced this initiative with great fanfare in June, 1997, but only after many years of intense public pressure. It then took almost eighteen months for the various parties to come to a specific agreement about what would be audited, who would do the auditing, and what type of report would be published. As a result of these delays and disagreements, the entire process is viewed by the public with great skepticism. As a matter of fact, two of the leading public interest group participants in the negotiations have refused to sign the new accord and have denounced it as too weak. Moreover, if experience to date is any indication, the implementation process is also likely to be subject to intense discussions among the participants, with resultant delays. Thus, it will be quite some time before anyone will have an opportunity to evaluate the importance and effectiveness of this code. The consequence of these failings has been further public antagonism and pressure on the corporations. Thus, rather than gaining public support and recognition for their efforts, the companies involved are being denounced for bad faith. There are also efforts to pursue legislative and regulatory approaches at national and international levels that would compel companies to undertake desired actions.

The Imperative of Global Codes of Conduct

Let me state categorically and unequivocally my belief that corporate codes of conduct are here to stay. Further, they are both necessary and desirable. When properly developed and implemented, codes of conduct can provide the corporation with a voluntary and flexible approach to addressing some of society's concerns, both in general and in the market-place. Codes can serve both corporate interests and public purposes and can strengthen free market institutions, as well. Effective use of codes can restore public faith in the market economy as the best avenue for enhancing human welfare, advancing regional economic development, and strengthening democratic institutions.

Public sentiment and perspective play a very important role in defining the parameters of discretion that a society will allow the leaders of its various social, political, and economic institutions. In the present instance, as well as in many previous instances involving social issues, the fight for the hearts and minds of the public have invariably been led by corporate critics. Companies, fearing lack of public trust, have refrained from a proactive stance and have instead limited themselves to disputing their critics' charges. This is a losing battle and will always remain so. By yielding the initiative to their critics, companies have allowed their critics to shape the agenda in ways that put business in a perpetually defensive mode, talking about "what they may have done wrong" instead of "what they are doing right."

Codes of conduct offer an invaluable opportunity for responsible corporations to create an individual and highly positive public identity for themselves; that is, a reputation effect that can have a direct result on their bottom line in terms of increased revenues, customer loyalty, expanded markets, a productive work force, and a supportive political and regulatory environment. Furthermore, an increased level of public confidence and trust among important constituencies and stakeholders would lead to greater freedom for management in the running of their business operations, and insulate them from the actions of other, less scrupulous firms in the market-place.

Voluntary codes serve to achieve a larger public purpose in a manner, that is flexible and pragmatic and take into account the unique set of problems faced by an industry or by different companies. *They* also allow the moderate elements among the affected groups to seek reasonable solutions to the issues involved, even before these issues are captured by more radical elements whose primary interest may be in escalating the level of social conflict, rather than fashioning mutually acceptable and feasible solutions.

And they avoid the need for further governmental regulation that is invariably more expensive and less efficient (because of political considerations and the need to create regulations that cover all possible situations and contingencies).

Creating a Code of Conduct

The remainder of this paper is devoted to a discussion of the development and implementation of a meaningful code of conduct for globally active corporations. This discussion will draw on my own experience as chair of the Mattel Independent Monitoring Council for Global Manufacturing Principles (MIMCO).

Characteristics of a Viable Code

A corporate code of conduct is in the nature of "private law" or a "promise voluntarily made," whereby an institution makes a public commitment to certain standards of conduct. The fact that issuance of a code is "voluntary" reflects the flexibility of action afforded to a corporation. Commitment to a code affirms that corporations and their critics share a common interest in improving the conditions of their interaction, and in mutually satisfactory resolution of underlying issues.

For a code of conduct to have any reasonable chance of meeting the expectations of all parties involved, the following conditions must be met.

- The code commitments must be economically viable for the corporation, given the dynamics of its technology and competition, and the economic and sociopolitical realities of the environments within which it operates.
- The code must address substantive issues that are of importance to the corporation's various constituencies, particularly employees, communities, and governments.
- The code must be specific about performance standards that can be objectively measured.
- Important constituencies of the corporation must be engaged in the code formulation and implementation process.

Development and Implementation

Development and implementation of a multinational code of conduct is a challenging task because of the differing orientations and concerns of the diverse parties involved; their disparate assumptions about the feasibility of particular goals and benchmarks; and disagreements about the means that are appropriate and feasible to achieve agreed-upon goals. Another major hurdle arises from the organizational ethos and decisionmaking processes of corporations and other participative and public interest groups. A corporation's primary focus is on the efficiency of processes and the optimization of outcomes. Participative and deliberative processes, e.g., open consultations and procedural norms, are adopted only as means to achieve desired ends and are not seen as values themselves. By contrast, many stakeholder groups place tremendous importance on consultation and information sharing, not only as steps in effective decision-making, but as values themselves. Thus, from their perspective, efficient use of time and resources may take second place to consultation and involvement; and corporate actions that appear to jeopardize participative processes are viewed with distrust.

Assuming that there is adequate commitment to widespread participation and involvement in code development, the next step is to determine the scope of the proposed code. This includes:

- Definition: What aspects of corporate activity and impact are to be included in the code?
- Measurement and Verification: How should corporate performance in these areas be measured, and how should the accuracy of this information be verified?
- Accountability and Reporting: To whom should the corporation be accountable for its performance, and how should this information be made public?

Specificity in all of these matters is critical because an ambiguous code tends either to become meaningless, or to expand into varied meanings as different groups stretch its terms to suit their particular interests. Code requirements must be translated into quantifiable and standardized measurements so that objective and consistent observations can be made by different people, over time. Code compliance must become an element of management routine that is integral, rather than peripheral, to the firm's normal operations. And, most importantly, indicators of code compliance must reflect results rather than intentions: goals met or unmet, not merely actions taken in pursuit of goals.

Two final points on implementation are these:

- The company's top management must be strongly and unequivocally committed to the code, and code compliance must be an

element of performance evaluation at all levels of management.
- The company must be willing to expose its record of code compli- ance to external verification. This last step is particularly important if the firm expects to achieve "reputation effects" and the benefits of stakeholder trust and collaboration, as well as public approval.

Independent Monitoring Systems

One of the most critical aspects of code implementation is the creation of an independent monitoring system. Independent monitoring is necessary for the public to see that companies are indeed doing what they proclaim to be doing. Unfortunately, most companies with codes are extremely reluctant to subject themselves to independent outside monitoring and public dis- semination of monitoring results.

This is an area of great disagreement between corporations and their crit- ics, and a major source of public distrust about corporate motives and per- formance. Reluctance to share information is sometimes justifiably based on the fear that the company will be subjected to inappropriate pressure and harassment, rather than be applauded for the progress it has made. However, inadequate disclosure inevitably suggests that there is some- thing to hide, and suggests a lack of faith in the ability of stakeholders to appreciate and encourage good corporate conduct. It is ironic that corpora- tions expect their financial performance to be publicly reported and audited by independent outsiders for the benefit of investors, but are unwilling to provide other information-often much less sensitive of com- parable concern to other vital constituencies.

Companies have often argued that many indicators of code compliance are internal measures, not conventionally subject to outside review, and that confidentiality makes it easier to take corrective actions through a sys- tem of "carrot and stick." This line of argument, however, has not been suc- cessful in previous situations involving crises of public confidence and is doomed to failure in the current global socio-political environment. Nei- ther advanced nor developing countries will allow companies to operate any longer under a "veil of secrecy" where issues of human rights and eth- ical/moral conduct are concerned.

There are currently two approaches to creating and implementing codes of conduct with appropriate performance verification and public reporting processes. One involves industry-wide effort; the other suggests that indi- vidual companies should develop their own approaches, based on their unique circumstances. We briefly consider the advantages and disadvan- tages of each.

Industry-Wide Effort

The case for an industry-wide effort is based on the premise that companies in an industry face similar sets of problems, competitive conditions, and external pressures. Therefore, a combined approach should be feasible, cost effective, and place all companies on the same competitive footing with respect to these issues. An industry-wide approach also gives participating companies a united position with which to respond to their critics and public at large.

There are, however, serious flaws to this logic:

- An industry-wide approach requires consensus before any action can be taken. It therefore plays into the hands of those companies who are least inclined to undertake substantive action, and thus can postpone implementation through endless discussion, procrastination and obfuscation, thereby defeating the purpose of the exercise and inviting public ridicule and distrust.
- It forces industry performance standards to the lowest common denominator; i.e., the company with the weakest record sets the pace for the entire industry.
- It reduces incentives for individual companies to improve their own performance based on their own particular circumstances.
- Since these industry-wide efforts invariably depend on "voluntary compliance" and rarely incorporate monitoring or enforcement measures, poorly performing companies remain undisciplined and taint the record of the entire industry.

I do not believe that, at the present time, an industry-wide approach is either feasible or desirable in most cases. Since very few industries have even a modicum of "commonly accepted" standards or performance criteria in *any* area of public concern, an effort to develop common performance criteria might appear to be-and might actually become-a form of anti-competitive collusion. Moreover, at the current stage of code development and public acceptance, an industry-wide approach is likely to be very disadvantageous to the companies that are seeking to develop creative, innovative responses to human and social concerns.

Independent Approach

I believe that for a company that is strongly committed to a substantive and effective code of conduct, a "go-it-alone" strategy is preferable at the present time. The direct economic benefits emanating from increased stakeholder trust, cooperation, and loyalty should provide ample incentive; and enhanced public reputation should translate into a more hospitable external socio-political environment over the long term. A go-it-alone company has the flexibility to fashion a code of conduct that takes advantage of its unique capabilities and to develop new systems and procedures of permanent value (and perhaps of market value to other firms as well). Successful individual firm experience may well permit the gradual development of multi-firm approaches.

Monitoring Council

Whatever the specific substantive content of a code of conduct, and whatever its level of sponsorship (division, corporate, or industry), its ultimate success depends upon the verification of its results by independent reviewers. I refer to these individuals as a "Monitoring Council." Such a Council should consist of three to five members with impeccable credentials for independence, knowledge, and, if possible, code formulation and implementation. The Council must have credibility with all constituent groups, including corporate directors and managers, governments, and other stakeholders. I do not believe that it is appropriate to include specific stakeholder representatives as Council members, since the Council's purpose is to determine the extent to which the company is meeting its public commitments, as expressed in its code. (Stakeholder representatives may well be included in consultations concerned with the drafting and revision of a code, which is a different matter.)

The principal task of a Monitoring Council should be oversight, with responsibility for verifying not only the results of field audits but, even more importantly, the company's responses to deficiencies when they are uncovered. Field monitoring of code compliance should be separated from verification and reporting, which should be the sole purview of the Council. The Council should develop a mechanism for receiving information and complaints about corporate performance from both within and outside the company. It should make regular public reports about the company's compliance with its code, and the content of these reports and the manner of their presentation should be the sole responsibility of the Council. The Council should, of course, make every effort to ensure that all facts in its reports are accurate, and that all conclusions are fully justified. Under the best of circumstances, the monitoring function should be viewed as a cooperative effort in which both the monitors and the corporation's field managers strive to ensure compliance. Under the worst of circumstances, where monitors and managers view each other as adversaries, the entire code implementation process will be a failure.

Mattel Experience

Mattel, the world's largest toy manufacturing company, announced the creation of its Global Manufacturing Principles (GMP) in November, 1997. The Code created a set of standards that would apply to all of the company-owned plants as well as those of its more than 300 primary contractor manufacturing facilities around the world. As part of its code formulation and implementation process, the company also committed itself to the establishment of an independent council to monitor its operations to ensure compliance with GMP. It is called the Mattel Independent Monitoring Council for Global Manufacturing Principles (MIMCO). To the best of my knowledge, it was the first time that a major multinational corporation voluntarily committed itself to independent monitoring by outside observers who had complete authority to make their findings available to the public.

In establishing the Council, Mattel was trying to identify itself as a socially responsible company and good corporate citizen. Mattel believed that it was important that its policies, operational procedures, and performance measures under the GMP should receive broad public recognition and acceptance. Mattel also considered it extremely important that the relevance and adequacy of the GMP, as applied to the company's overseas operations, particularly in developing countries, be recognized and accepted by its employees and managers worldwide.

The Council currently consists of three members: Dr. S. Prakash Sethi, Distinguished University Professor of Management, Zicklin School of Business, City University of New York; Dr. Murray Weidenbaum, Distinguished University Professor of Economics, Washington University in St. Louis, and a former chairman of the Council of Economic Advisors; and Dr. Paul McCleary, President and CEO of ForChildren, Inc., and former President and CEO of the Save the Children Foundation.

In accepting their assignment, Council members received a number of important assurances from the company's top management:

- Mattel will ensure that the code meets or exceeds all pertinent host country laws and best industry practices in the areas of its operations.
- The company is committed to the code and will devote the necessary resources to ensure compliance to it by field managers in the company's owned and controlled plants, and will cooperate and assist the company's major vendors to comply with the code.

- The company will create a highly objective, quantifiable, and out-come-oriented set of standards that will add substance and comprehensiveness to the code and ensure the code's implementation in a meaningful manner.
- The company will make every effort to work toward the enhancement of these standards in an evolutionary manner that will enhance the financial and social well-being of its workers, and also contribute to the economic growth of the countries involved.

During its first phase, MIMCO will focus its efforts on auditing those twenty or more plants that are owned or controlled by Mattel. These account for close to 70 percent of Mattel's world-wide production. A very large part of Mattel's production operations are based in the Asia-Pacific Region: Peoples' Republic of China, Indonesia, and Malaysia. This audit will therefore cover the topics that have been of major public concern in those areas: workers' health and safety, wages, and living conditions. We expect this phase of the audit process to be completed by April 1999, and our findings will be made public soon thereafter.

An audit is only as good as the questions it asks and the activities and issues it covers. We have spent the last six months developing a highly objective, quantifiable, precise, and statistically rigorous set of instruments that will be used in conducting field audits. These will cover, among other things:

- Workers' environment, health and safety, and working conditions.
- Wages and working hours.
- Living conditions.
- Communications with the management concerning their living and working conditions, new employee orientation methods, and regular training programs.

Mattel has already completed extensive in-house audits to ensure that its own plants, and those of its major suppliers, are in compliance with GMP. Where necessary, it has also worked closely with the company's suppliers to help them improve their operations to meet Mattel's standards – frequently at Mattel's expense. And, in a number of cases, where suppliers have been unable or unwilling to make such an effort, Mattel has discontinued its business relationship with them. Mattel has established a single global task force with members located in its Asian Region headquarters in Hong Kong and in its corporate headquarters in El Segundo, California. This task *force* has been responsible for generating the necessary databases for Council use in creating audit protocols; these, in turn, will be used by the independent auditors appointed by, and reporting to, the Council.

Concluding Thoughts

The emerging global economic order of the 1990s has once again brought capitalism and its principal actor, the multinational corporation, to new levels of prominence and power. Unlike the 1960s, when multinational corporations were seen as a threat to national sovereignty and political freedom, the dominant contemporary view seems to be that the multinational corporation is – or certainly can be – an agent of positive change. However, beneath this veneer of hope and expectation, lies distrust in the unaccountability of the corporate behemoth and the fear of its potential for doing harm whether through misjudgment or abuse of power.

The contemporary tensions between business and society – which will certainly extend into the next millennium – do not arise from obvious conflicts between right and wrong, guilt or innocence. Their more subtle sources are, for example, alternative concepts and combinations of equity and inequity, the distribution of potential social and economic benefits, the virtue of frugality and the sin of undue accumulation, and the morality of principles versus the morality of situations. We realize that we live in an increasingly interdependent, global society where the welfare of the individual human being is deeply, and often unpredictably, embedded in the operation of the entire system. In this complex environment, we cannot pretend to separate moral principles from institutional practices, political power from economic influence, or human and environmental values from material wealth.

The large corporation must become an active agent for social change if it is to make the world safe for itself. Rules of law, democratic institutions, and the ethics of competition and the marketplace are requirements for the continued success of multinational corporations and, indeed, contemporary capitalism. The corporation can no longer pretend to be a reactive participant within the social system, responding (positively or negatively) to pressures and goals arising from other groups. As a dominant institution in society, it must accept responsibility for independent initiative, both with respect to its own goals and the formation of the public agenda. Effective participation requires that the corporation be able to articulate who and what it is from a social perspective, and what role its processes and products play in society. This articulation is, in fact, the ultimate purpose and result of a corporate code of conduct.

David Selley, "Bribing foreign government officials now illegal," _management ethics_ (February 1999): 1–3. Also available online at: http://www.ethicscentre.ca/EN/resources/February%201999%20methics .pdf

In December the federal government passed the _"Corruption of Foreign Public Officials Act"_ (the Act) which, effective in mid February, makes it a criminal offence punishable by up to five years in jail to pay a bribe to a foreign public official to gain a business advantage. The media either didn't notice or chose to remain silent. By most estimates Canadian companies are not aware of this Act and the effect it may have on the way they do business. In late 1997, the 28 OECD member countries had approved a Convention that would outlaw major bribery of government officials and, according to Milos Barutciski, a lawyer with Toronto law firm Davies Ward & Beck, the Canadian legislation has done a good job in implementing the requirements of that convention. Barutciski chaired a Canadian Bar Association Task Force on International Corruption that provided input to, and support for, the Canadian implementation of the Convention. So what previously has been a business and an ethical issue, now also becomes a legal issue for Canadian companies and their officers and directors. In fact, it has always been a legal issue in the countries in which a bribe has been paid. There is no country in the world where bribery of public officials is legal, or publicly acceptable. One has only to look at the current travails of the International Olympic Committee (IOC), and the developing revelations in Indonesia. What is new with this Act is that bribing a foreign government official is now illegal in Canada broadly in the same way it would be illegal to pay a bribe to a Canadian government official.

The Act covers loans, awards and advantages of any other kind made directly or indirectly to a government official to obtain a business advantage by inducing that official to act or refrain from acting in some way. Government officials include elected officials and others. Governments include political subdivisions of countries, government agencies and also international organizations formed by governments.

A typical case might be paying an agent to assist in obtaining a government contract to, say, build a dam, and instructing the agent to use some of the funds to bribe a government official to award the contract to their principal, rather than to another bidder. Of course, if the other bidders bribe too, this will become a mug's game for all bidders. The Act also makes it an offence to deal in the proceeds of bribery and clarifies that any payment that falls within the ambit of this Act is not deductible for income tax purposes. Finally, the Act exempts "facilitating payments" to junior public

The Centre at Ten Years Old

"The whole objective of the Centre has been to shake our society of its complacency, to question a status quo that too often accepts as inevitable those activities which are bad not only for our moral character, but for the bottom line as well."

The Centre held its 10th anniversary celebration on December 2, 1998 at the Royal Bank of Canada where special recognition was given to the Centre's founding directors. David Olive, a founding director himself and senior writer with *The National Post*, gave a tribute to the achievements of the past ten years to about 70 of the Centre's past and present corporate and individual supporters, as well as many former and current directors. He lauded the progress that the Centre has made over the past decade in bringing issues to light. "We've made the forceful point that ethics isn't an arcane set of rules. It is merely an appreciation of the consequences of behaviour that may bring regret and injury to ourselves and others." He described the Centre as "part of the vanguard" that has raised the level of moral tolerance and sounded a call to action. David also reminded us that much needs to be done. He challenged the Centre "to be more aggressive in identifying soul-destroying ethical lapses, and the chronic ethical abuses that still characterise too many aspects of business life." He concluded by saying he was excited by the prospect of the Centre's growing role as a forum for ideas and solutions in a world far more attuned to ethical values than ten years ago. Sincere thanks are due to The Royal Rank for use of their outstanding premises for our celebration.

officials that are demanded in order to perform tasks of a routine nature, such as issuing vehicle or business licences, or import and export documentation which are common in many countries. While such practices are generally harmful to the countries concerned, they are not easy to eliminate in the short term. From the point of view of the OECD Convention and the Act they can be argued to not confer a business advantage because all businesses pay these amounts as a matter of course. Like all legislation, there will be opportunities for differing interpretations and room for loopholing, but the wording is strong and unequivocal in its primary thrust – elimination of major bribery and corruption by Canadians of foreign officials for business advantage.

The OECD Convention, and the Canadian Act, resulted from the strenuous efforts of many multi-national businesses, governments and NGOs, particularly Transparency International (TI), a non-profit international organization based in Berlin whose mission is to get rid of major bribery in international business transactions. TI has fought for this legislation for many years in many countries. Professor Wes Cragg of the Schulich School of Business at York University is president of the Canadian Chapter of TI. He is proud of TI's pivotal role internationally, and in Canada in persuading the government to push the legislation through before the December 31 deadline. This was critical to the success of the entire OECD initiative because the Convention was required to be ratified by five major countries in order to become effective, and Canada was the last of the five to sign on. The Bill was passed quickly by the Senate and then zipped through all three readings in the House of Commons in one day.

Cragg and other proponents of the Act recognize that legislation, even in the 28 OECD countries and the handful of others that have signed on voluntarily, cannot stop the practice, but because these signatories account for approximately 80% of world trade a significant reduction in bribery is anticipated. Previously, some Canadian businesspersons and their advisors have been somewhat cynical about this issue; they have taken the approach that they would of course rather not pay a bribe, but that's the only way business can be done in some countries. In most cases they will now think twice (at least) before doing something that could send them to jail for five years. For many, hopefully most, the mere fact that it is illegal will dissuade them from participating. Most companies' codes of ethics start with the requirement that they will comply with the law!

Michael Davies, vice-president and general counsel for GE Canada, a strong proponent of the OECD Convention and heavily involved in its development, believes that many large Canadian companies have in recent years developed codes of conduct that include prohibitions against paying major bribes. Many companies, he said, including GE, walk away from deals because they are unwilling to pay bribes. Such companies may simply need to reinforce their current codes by stressing the illegality of what before had merely been contrary to their code. However, Davies believes an educational effort may be necessary for other companies that operate in this environment so that they are aware of the Act and are helped to understand the issues involved. The lack of media coverage to date has not helped. The Financial Post finally published an editorial on the Act on January 20th. It was not entirely favourably inclined to the legislation. On the other hand, The Economist (January 16th) devoted a strongly supportive editorial and a three page article to the coming into force of the Convention. This is consistent with the Economist's editorial stance in favour, except in exceptional circumstances, of unfettered free markets and trade. Paying bribes to obtain or retain business has been a major impediment to the smooth operation of markets and flow of trade and can seriously distort outcomes, to the detriment of everyone except the recipients of the bribes and their Swiss or other off-shore bankers.

Why would big business be so much in favour of this initiative? After all, large companies are not associated in the public's mind with asking for more rules. In addition to ethical considerations, though, big business is looking for a level playing field. The United States has had legislation banning foreign bribery for many years. US companies said they were put at a competitive disadvantage when bidding on major contracts against competitors from Germany, France, Britain and other home bases for multi-national business, including Canada. Now the playing field will be level for most of the world that exports capital investment and business.

Or will it? Legislation is one thing; enforcement is another. The OECD Convention requires signatories to establish a monitoring and reporting process on enforcement. The Canadian Act requires the Ministers of Foreign Affairs, International Trade and Justice to report annually to Parliament on implementation of the convention – an unusual provision that should be interesting to watch. Cragg points out that TI is strongly urging the OECD to develop its own effective monitoring mechanisms to ensure member countries enforce the Act. If some major countries do not live up to their commitment the overall effect of the Convention will be drastically reduced, not only because companies from those countries may continue to pay bribes but because then companies from other countries will lose competitiveness if they do not follow suit – the level playing field will have been ploughed up.

Compliance within companies is not guaranteed either. For example, nobody pretends that the US Foreign Corrupt Practices Act has stopped all bribery by US companies nor that codes of conduct that prohibit bribes are always effective. There are, however, other mechanisms that may discourage the kinds of bribes covered by this Act. Senior management and boards of directors will likely become more conscious of situations in which they, or their subsidiaries in other countries, may be asked for a bribe. They may become more sensitive about unusually large agency fees. Companies that do business in high risk areas will consider the potential for illegal bribes in their risk management processes, if they did not before. For public companies, their auditors have to change the way they look at evidence that bribes covered by this Act may have been paid. Now that they are illegal, they are covered by the requirements of generally accepted auditing standards that relate to illegal acts. Auditors must understand their client's business sufficiently to be able to assess the risk of breaches of laws and regulations that might materially affect the financial statements. According to Diana Hillier, Director of Assurance Standards for the Canadian Institute of Chartered Accountants (CICA), this would require an auditor of a company with major business transactions in high risk countries to be alert for evidence that illegal bribes may have been paid. Auditors are not required to design procedures to investigate whether any have been paid, however, unless they find evidence that makes them suspicious, such as an unusually large agency fee. If auditors find evidence that an illegal bribe has been, or might have been paid, they must first assess whether the consequences may be material to the financial statements. Often they would not be, but even in this case CICA standards require the auditors to report the matter to senior management and the board, and if they are not satisfied that appropriate action has been taken the standards suggest seeking legal advice on their options. Large public accounting firms will no doubt be informing their audit personnel about the Act, and building awareness into their audit processes.

In short, the OECD Convention, and the Canadian Act are an important first step that can have only positive effects. With strict enforcement by the OECD countries, large scale bribery of foreign public officials will significantly diminish and provide a strong incentive for companies to resist pressure to pay bribes. It must be recognized, however, that there are a few major players that have not signed on (Hong Kong and Singapore, for example) and if individual companies, or entire industries, continue to believe they must pay bribes to get the business they need to stay alive, they will probably be able to find ways of hiding the bribes and loopholing the law. Only time will tell whether this seriously detracts from the effectiveness of the Convention and Act. For now, though, we can rejoice that a major step has been taken that might eventually rid the world of this scourge on international business and on domestic economies.

> Companies that do business in high risk areas will consider the potential for illegal bribes in their risk management processes...

If you are involved in any way in international business, it is relatively easy to arm yourself with two key pieces of information about this issue. The first is the Act itself (also known as Bill S-21), which consists of only six short paragraphs, the related amendment to the Income Tax Act, and a few other amendments that only lawyers need to worry about. The second vital piece of information is TI's so-called "Corruption Perception Index", based on the perception by business executives of which countries are the most susceptible to bribery. This index is widely publicized, and is available from TI Canada's web site, www.bus.yorku.ca/program/TranIntl/index .htm, or from TI's main site at www.transparency.de. If you are doing business with government officials or their agents in countries at or near the bottom of TI's list, you ought to take special steps to ensure that your company is not breaking Canadian law.

Beneficiaries of the OECD convention, if it works, will include: companies in Canada and other OECD nations whose codes of ethics and values have prevented them from paying bribes and who have walked away from deals that other less scrupulous companies have won; companies and their owners, who will no longer have to bear the cost of paying the bribes, or inflated agency fees; the ordinary people in countries low on the TI index whose economies have been distorted and rendered less efficient because of misallocation of resources; employees on the front line of international business transactions who will be under less pressure, or will have added support to resist; and international organizations such as the World Bank and IMF whose efforts to deal with financial problems of the developing world will be less distorted by diversion into off-shore bank accounts of moneys that should have gone to development. A few, though, will lose a great deal. We should not shed any tears for them.

David Selley, FCA is past-chair and a director of the Canadian Centre for Ethics & Corporate Policy and a consultant in auditing standards, methodologies and technologies.

Graham Tucker, "Ethical analysis for environmental problem solving,"
Agenda for Action Conference Proceedings, the Canadian Centre for
Ethics & Corporate Policy, 1990, 53–57.

Introduction

Today, no company can claim to be "ethical" unless it is demonstrating a
concern for the environment. The focus of this conference is on the tools of
ethical analysis and problem solving that can provide a practical framework for action.

Before finalizing a business decision, an executive should ask a series of
questions designed to ensure the best possible choice is made both for the
shareholders as well as other stakeholders. These questions ought to be
asked in the following order to canvass the values shown:

1. Is it profitable? (market values)
2. Is it legal? (legal values)
3. Is it fair? (social values)
4. Is it right? (personal values)
5. Is it sustainable development (environmental values)

These questions have been built into the "five-box" framework for ethical analysis which is shown in Figure 1.

Figure 1 Questions

The focus on values is critical to the proper analysis of business decisions
because morality, which is becoming more and more critical to the health of
corporations and society, cannot be legislated. It depends on the value
system of corporate leaders and employees. Moreover, the tough choices
required among alternatives often defy quantification and must be based
on the values of the decision-maker.

Nowadays, it is not safe to judge a propsective action just on its
contribution to profits, because the action may not be legal. Even if it is
profitable and legal, society will penalize the company if the action is not
also perceived to be fair and right. Recently, as the fragility of our global
environment has become clear, society has begun to demand that corporate
actions fit into the sustainable development of our economy.

The application of the "five-box" framework for analysis will be
developed below in the analysis of the Kardell Paper Co. case, after a

discussion of some terms used in ethical analysis and the outlining of a framework for ethical problem solving.

Some Important Distinctions

It's important that we make important distinctions (a) between management and leadership and (b) between being legal and being ethical. Lack of clear distinction in these areas causes a lot of confused thinking in business ethics.

When managers are successful, usually it is because they are high-energy, hard-driving individuals who know how to play by the rules of the game. They efficiently and single-mindedly strive to achieve the goals of the organization. But they may or may not be leaders.

Robert Greenleaf, author of the book *Servant Leadership*, defines leaders as "those who better see the path ahead and are prepared to take the risks and show the way." The characteristic which sets leaders apart from managers is their intuitive insight and the foresight which enables them to go out ahead and show the way. Why would anyone accept the leadership of another, except that the other sees more clearly where it's best to go? The manager, by contrast, tends to be part of the bureaucracy that wants to preserve the status quo. The managerial role determines the values. Managers do what's expected of them. That role often overrides the managers' personal values.

Role responsibility can be very powerful. The management of Johns-Manville knew for years that its product asbestos was linked by scientists to lung cancer in its employees. Similar situations existed with the Ford Pinto and the Dalkon Shield.

Managers often feel powerless to act outside of their prescribed role; they feel that they don't have the authority to buck the system. The corporate authority may be sanctioning the unethical behavior. It takes the moral authority of a leader to change the system, and this is often notably lacking in both politics and business.

Robert Greenleaf points out that the failure of businesspeople to use foresight and take creative action before a crisis arises is tantamount to *ethical failure*, because managers in these cases lack courage to act when there is still some freedom to change course. Many managers opt for short-term profit at the expense of long-term viability. On that basis there are probably a lot of people walking around with an air of innocence which they would not have if society were able to pin the label "unethical" on them for their failure to foresee crises and to act constructively when there was freedom to act.

Figure 1
A Framework for Ethical Analysis – Changing Ground Rules and a Sustainable Future

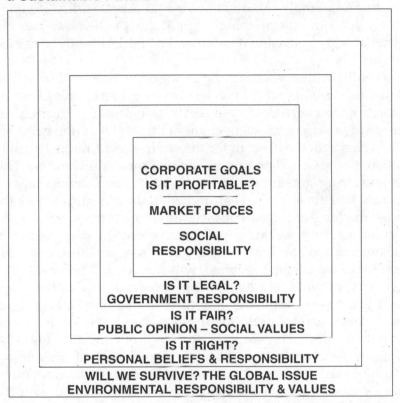

Similarly, it is important that we distinguish between being legal and being ethical. The law is frequently quite distinct from morality. It is mainly concerned with the minimum regulation required for public order, whereas ethics attempts to achieve what is "best" for both the individual and society. Thus it's possible to be operating within the law and yet be unethical. The legal limits for a certain pollutant may have been established before it was discovered to be unsafe at that level. The company may be operating legally. Yet by knowingly endangering the health of workers or the community, the company is acting in an unethical manner.

Many corporate codes of ethics express a commitment to keeping the letter of the law, but that may not protect them from censure when the new data becomes public knowledge. Obviously we have to have laws and regulations to avoid the chaos of a lawless society. However, the ethical crunch that is being experienced by the business world today is that the communications revolution is putting more information in the hands of the public. It used to be possible to exercise power and control by withholding or concealing information. If you don't know that asbestos dust is giving you lung cancer you can't do anything about it. The public now finds out very quickly what is going on, and it is demanding ethical conduct because this affects its well-being.

We have recently witnessed dramatic changes in Eastern Europe, as shared information has empowered previously powerless people to rise up and take control of their own destiny in seeking a better life. Precisely the same power is at work in our society, changing the rules of the game for business. Five years ago, the concern for the environment ranked sixth in the value system of the Canadian public. Today it ranks number one. This in turn is empowering government to enact much tougher regulations. Those companies that are either too entrenched in the old rules or lack the foresight to see the long-term consequences of what is now perceived by the public to be unethical behavior will fail. Whereas those companies which use a combination of ethical foresight and good business and have the courage to make the changes required, will survive and prosper.

Legislation may provide a level playing field, but legislation alone cannot solve the problem. Similarly, strong corporate statements about environmental values also are useless if business does not have the ethical will to comply with them. The health of our environment depends more than anything else upon corporate moral leadership, which reflects the personal values of executives and employees. And this is where we move from theory to the realm of applied ethics, which is concerned with the practical outcome of business decisions.

Value Judgments

The name of the game is making value judgments in the light of our personal values. I want to say a few words about values so that we can have a common language in this conference.

Values are the criteria by which we make our judgments or choices, and establish our goals and priorities. For most of us, there is a bit of a gap between our ideal personal values and our actual or operative values, and we need to be honest about what our values really are.

The situation is complicated for us today as social values are changing, and this is redefining ethical standards. The ground rules are changing.

Studies have shown the following characteristics resulting from people having clear or unclear values:

A FRAMEWORK FOR ETHICAL PROBLEM SOLVING

Consider the following issues while employing the eight steps listed below:

1. Establish objectivity.
Who is doing the analysis and what interests do they represent?

What are the ground rules of the company and of the decision-making group?

2. Scan the situation; identify the problem.
Separate out the "core problem" from the subproblems. Whose problem is it? Why is it a problem?

3. Analyse the problem.
Use the "five-box," or "five-question" framework (the chart on the following page) to analyze the situation. What are the operative ground rules or values from the perspective of corporation's existing rules, as well as the legal, public, personal and environmental implications. Who makes the decision? Who are the stakeholders? What are their ground rules? Is it fair to all concerned?

4. Determine the cause of the problem.
Why and how are the rules being broken? Are the rules being broken Prima facie or Categorical? Is there any justification? Specify the cause.

5. Establish the objective.
Describe the desirable outcome, or end-point. Is it achievable? How would you measure it? What is the time frame?

6. Explore the options.
Brainstorm possible solutions. Create alternative courses of action.

7. Decide on the best solution.
Who will be affected by each option? Evaluate the impacts from each option on each group of stakeholders. Which option maximizes the benefits and minimizes the burden? Will it pass the five-box ethics test?

8. Plan and implement the solution.

Unclear values	Clear values
Apathetic	Know who they are
Flighty	Know what they want
Inconsistent	Positive
Drifter	Purposeful
Role player	Enthusiastic
Indecisive	Decisive

Both individually and corporately, it is to our advantage to develop a clear set of values, because confused values will result in confused ethical decisions.

Ethical analysis usually uncovers value conflicts which occur below the surface of our thinking. They can't be settled by rational argument. Only as we listen respectfully to each other's value perspective is it possible to find a reasonable accommodation of the difference. This is why stakeholder analysis is so important.

Rule Ethics

This brings us to the two basic ethical concepts we will apply in our case study today. The first is rule ethics.

Rule ethics states that you make your decisions about right or wrong on the basis of valid ethical principles, norms or ground rules. In other words, we ask, "Will this proposed action be violating civil law, or company policy in the code of ethics?" This is a good place to start, but as mentioned before, it may not produce ethical decisions. The decisions that result may be legal – but if the ground rules have changed, they may not be ethical.

The next level of Rule Ethics consists of the the rules or principles that come out of our moral traditions, which in our society are mainly the Judeo Christian moral norms such as "Thou shalt not kill, steal, lie, cheat or oppress."

The underlying question in Rule Ethics is, Whose rules are you following? It used to be that the corporation had its own rules, which related only to market forces, and it was not felt to be necessary to consider the values of society. That is, "What's good for General Motors is good for the rest of us." Cynically, the Golden Rule has become, "He who has the gold makes the rules."

Utilitarianism, Or End-point Ethics

John Stuart Mill said that, "To determine whether an action is right or wrong, one must concentrate on its likely consequences – the end point or end result. What is the greatest benefit for the greatest number?"

This led to cost-benefit analysis: does the benefit justify the cost? And to risk-benefit analysis: does the benefit justify the business risk?

In other words, you begin with Rule Ethics, in which the stakeholders test a decision by asking:

Is it legal?
Is it fair?
Is it right?
Is it environmentally sound?

Then you move to the end-point ethics, which seeks the greatest benefit for the greatest number – and this, finally, forces us to make some trade-offs to achieve the greatest good.

So far, we have been considering the process of ethical analysis. However, there is a tendency to think that having analyzed the problem we have solved it. Unless we take it to the next step of rational problem solving, nothing much is – going to happen.

The process I am going to introduce is ethically neutral. The thing that makes it ethical is the particular values and ground rules you apply in the process. If the ethical analysis has been done thoroughly, you will have already sorted out the values that you will apply at the various decision points in the problem-solving process.

Creative problem solving involves lateral thinking, or second-order thinking.

First-order thinking is the obvious course of action that first occurs to the mind of the manager or executive.

Second-order thinking involves "refraining" the problem and considering it from a different perspective.

For example, if you look at a business problem from the perspective of each of the five boxes on the chart, you might generate some creative alternatives which might not come to mind if only the corporate box is considered. It will take courage for every business enterprise to make the ethical shift for a sustainable future, but some can and *are* leading the way.

Graham H. Tucker was founder and Director of the King-Bay Chaplaincy in Toronto, and acting executive director of the Canadian Centre for Ethics and Corporate Policy. Mr. Tucker was author of The *Faith-Work Connection*.